The Gospel of You

The Truth about God, Religion, and Who You Really Are

Also by Jarrad Hewett

Love, Life, God:

The Journey of Creation

The Big E – Everything is Energy

The Gospel of You

*The Truth about God, Religion,
and Who You Really Are*

By Jarrad Allen Hewett

This book is not intended to be considered legal, medical, or any other professional service. The information provided is not a substitute for

professional advice or care. If you require or desire legal, medical, or other expert assistance, you should seek such service. The author, the publisher, and their employees and agents are not liable for any damages

arising from or in connection with the use of or reliance on any information contained in this book.

Legacy Publications First Edition - September 2011

Love to All

Contents

Preface

I was hanging out with my family down in beautiful Newport Beach, California, strolling along through the little boutiques just off of Pacific Coast Highway, when I found myself face to face with John Lennon. He was papered behind a large display of denim just next to the epic words of his hit song, "Imagine." As I read the words, I had this wonderful realization that John's song embodied the greatest message Source has for us all: You are the wonderfully loved creators of your Universe. You are love, and you are all that is. Now, John didn't exactly say it like that, but as I read the words, "no hell below us," and "a brotherhood of man" I couldn't help but feel the connection to my own pure, positive Source. I continued reading "sharing all the world," "living for today."

"Yes!" I thought. "That's how it's done."

A tear came to my eye as I took in the beauty and synchronicity of this experience. There I'd been, just a few weeks earlier, pondering the continuation of my next book. Now, face to face with John Lennon, I was looking at my answer.

At this point, my family had moved on to the next store, so I said "thank you" to Mr. Lennon, and "thank you" to the Universe, and I walked down the street and into the next shop. Imagine my surprise when not even a minute after walking in, "Imagine" started playing in the store.

I couldn't help but laugh. Just in case I hadn't *really* gotten it, here it was again: Imagine. In that moment, I heard it in the lyrics of a song. A few moments before, I'd seen it on a poster and felt it in an idea.

You may see it in a blade of grass, or the sparkling eyes of a child. Some may believe it is peace, while others spread war and death in its name.

Some people dedicate their whole lives to finding it, while others spend life times denying it any existence at all.

It doesn't matter what you call this thing through which miracles are born, wars declared, and for which men, women, and children will live and die… but imagine for a second, you called it you.

From the beginning of time, humanity has asked the questions, "Who am I?" "What does it all mean?" "Why am I here?"

As a collective consciousness, we've been searching for thousands and thousands of years for a better understanding of God, and we've looked everywhere except the one place we're most sure of finding the answers – within ourselves.

Jesus Himself was asked where the kingdom of heaven was. He didn't reply, "Well, when you die, you go off to this wonderful place." He simply said of the kingdom, "You will not say "Look. There is the Kingdom. For the Kingdom of heaven lies within."

You are just one of the many mansions within that vast kingdom called Source.

Can you imagine?

Well, that's what I'm going to ask you to do as you read this book. I'm going to ask you to imagine for a moment, that everything in this world is energy. I'm going to ask you for a moment, to set aside your beliefs and really look at this wonderful place we call earth, and imagine you are the creator of it all.

Introduction

You have asked who we are, and we have come forward to say that we are you. We are of the Allness that you are. It is no coincidence that you have chosen to begin this work as Passover approaches, because for millennia, mankind has held that he must please an outside source, lest he not be "passed" over and experience damnation and destruction. We are here to tell you that no one will ever suffer eternal damnation, for how could God condemn what God is?

Your religions have taught you separation; yet we have come to tell you that you are not bound to the ideology of those whose experiences have come before. Does consciousness not evolve? Are you not born into this physical embodiment as a child and grow from there? Such has been consciousness on your plane. We are coming forward now, because you have come forward now. Consciousness has chosen to rise above limitation and remember the truth of who we are. We are here because we have asked to expand out from our limited perspective and into the full light of the one true god – whom we all are.

The man you know as Jesus spoke of love. When asked of his presence on this plane he responded, "I

13

have come that the Father might be in me, and I in you, that All may know they are one." He came to deliver the consciousness of truth to the seekers. Those who understood this message continued in their understanding. Consciousness at that point was not ready to fully embody his words. Yet, his truth did not die out. It did not go away. It has been here with you all along.

He went to prepare a place for you, and that place is the kingdom of heaven that exists within each and every one of us. It is the consciousness of truth made manifest. This consciousness did not ascend with a physical Christ. It has been here all along, waiting to be called forth for understanding and application.

Those who wrote you religious texts were indeed inspired by god, yet they were limited in their understanding of who this "god" is. These men (and in some cases women) were not Saints to be praised or people to be worshipped. They were simply beings who chose to come forward and experience life - just as you are. They had no more of a connection to the divine than you, for all are divine. Their desire to know themselves was just as inspired as the ancients. The things they channeled are in many cases wonderful teachings, yet your consciousness has evolved and is ready for a new understanding in some cases, and a completely new experience in others.

The story of religion has simply become the story of As religion took hold – as has been the case with all religion where god is placed outside of the self – man simply forgot his connection. He was told it was wrong – of the devil. This was not a "wrong" thing, for in the mind of god, all possibilities are welcome. There is no judgment here because to judge the actions of any is to judge the actions of the one. Within creation, there is never a moment of separation. We're simply here to help change the story and move consciousness into an even larger truth about unity and love.

You've asked of us a specific task. You've asked that we come forward with an understanding that can bridge the new and the old. We say to you that the easiest way to grasp that which you think of as "the new," is to simply let go of what you term "the old." As Einstein wonderfully channeled, "You cannot solve a problem with the same mind that created it."

However, understanding that you wish for this to be an explanation and exploration of consciousness over time – that is to say the evolving consciousness and it's seemingly "paradoxical" relationship with religion and that which you have called God - we wish for you to know that we are here, and we are indeed ready to help you as you usher in that which you are. You are the consciousness of Christ, the mind of god, the creator of your "new" earth; indeed, you are creation itself.

Chapter 1

The Beginning

Man has battled his own knowingness for most of your recorded history – and even beyond. There was a time when man walked this plane as conscious creator, but eventually, the separated mind – the ego – convinced him that he was in fact separate from the individualized source of all. The Allness and Unity was forgotten, and was replaced with the notions of "survival" and "other." This layout is presented wonderfully in the story of Eden. However, we have titled this chapter "The Beginning," and we wish to start there.

There was no beginning, only a separation – and even then, this separation was only an illusion. The God that you are set in motion a thought that allowed for the individualized experience of all that God is from a perception of being "other." Those who wrote your Bible illustrate this in the very first verse. "In the beginning God created the heavens and the earth." These are the first words of the Bible, yet they do not begin with a beginning as such. They begin with man's birth into separation. Genesis does not begin at the beginning, because as we have said, there was no beginning.

God has always existed. Indeed, you have always existed. The Biblical story of creation was created by a human mind searching for an understanding of its place on this plane. Man knew that he was, but he did not know how he came to be. He externalized his authorship and gave his creation away to a god made in his image. The Bible tells you that you are made in God's image, and indeed that is true, but the image most think of when they think of God is an image made in the likeness of man. The one true Source has always been, and thus, the beginning was no beginning at all. If we call it energy, you can understand it in a more detached, yet specific way. Energy is neither created nor destroyed. All that is, has always been. It simply manifests in ever-changing ways. Thus is the story of you.

Quantum physics phrases it this way: "That which is focused upon appears." Man had an innate knowing of this as it appears not just in your creation story, but in many, many others. The Bible says that "the world was without form," and indeed it was – just as all potential is without form. Form comes into being from a thought which has been focused upon. In this case, your world came into being once you as God focused upon it.

This Biblical version of creation existed long before it was adopted by the Israelites and added to the Torah. The Israelites were slaves for many years, and they borrowed heavily from the customs of their captors, the Egyptians. Such is the literal explanation for many of the stories in mythology – be they Christian, Greek, Roman, or other; yet there is more at play. There is a deeper meaning in much of the Bible, and in much of all world religions. In other words, beyond what the mind has mentalized, conceptualized, and authorized, lies the truth.

Take for example, the spirit of God moving upon the waters. What are you?

Water.

Indeed. This is an allusion to how you came into being as an individualized self, free to experience God as "other." It is the creation story of your individualized self. You are the energy or spirit that moved upon the waters of creation. You are the energy that created your individualized self – the self which you perceive as separate.

As we have said, there was a time when man walked this plane as conscious creator, but eventually, the separated mind – the ego – convinced him that he was the sole inhabitant of his world. Therefore, something must have come before.

Man walked with God in the garden of paradise until he was tempted to eat of the tree of knowledge.

Metaphorically, that tree represents the ego, which separates from God – not because the ego is evil, but because it is the mechanism through which man experiences himself as separate. It is the part of you that defines itself as temporary; that is all. This only becomes a "problem" when the temporary wishes to become permanent. We'd also like to add, that the temporary is not actually temporary. When you die, you do not actually die. You expand. You become all that you are. Therefore, in a way, there is a death, but the death is only of the illusion. Religion has been created by the illusion. End of story.

Wow… Can you describe why or how that story came about?

Not knowing what you know, what story would you have created to justify your hardships? The politics between nations and gender are not new to this plane. Women were viewed as lower than men, and thus, the story which was written by man of his creation reflected that belief. God is man, yet God uses woman to create His offspring. Energy becomes split along gender lines, and while both are given purpose, they are also given roles and fall into a hierarchy which explains and sets forth a template for society.

What about the devil's role in this separation? The Bible tells us that he took on the role of a serpent and tempted Eve?

Mankind was not able to accept responsibility for creation, therefore "Satan" came forth as the entity upon which mankind could lay the blame for its own "faults." There had to be some reason man was not God. There had to be something to blame for separation in this system of hierarchy and law. You know this from your history of the Bible.

You mean linguistically?

Indeed.

Well, I know that if you take the scriptures literally, then you believe that God made Adam and Eve without sin, but that Romans 8:20-21 says, "For the creature (us) was made subject to vanity not willingly, but by reason of Him (God) Who hath subjected the same in hope. Because the creature itself also shall be delivered from the bondage of corruption into the glorious liberty of the children of God." If you take the Bible literally, then this means that God meant for us to be the way we are.

Indeed, <u>You</u> meant for you to be the way you are.

Yes, but I'm speaking strictly from a Biblical point of view.

So are we. You see? Apply what you know to be true. You are the creator who has chosen to have this experience. If you view yourself as separate from God, it is not a wrong choice on your part; it is simply a choice you have made. When you choose to remember of whom you are (God) you will be "delivered." You will once again know your true nature. Thus is the essence of that passage.

This makes sense when you look at Romans 11:36 which says, "For of Him, and through Him, and to Him, are all things."

Indeed. There is no separation. The problem many have with relation to this knowledge is that they are choosing to see a tree instead of a forest. It enables them to continue to play their game of "I am God/I am not God," or, "There is only One God, and it is a God of jealousy and anger and I must serve that God, not this God… which must be fake, therefore evil!" You see, many ask, yet when they receive the answer, they say, "but how can this be?" The answer is, it is, just as all things are. You may accept whatever you choose and thus shall be your reality.

Proverbs 23:7 "As a man thinketh in his heart, so is he."

Indeed. Buddha and many more masters taught the same. They were disregarded by some, because they were teaching a way that appeared to be different from the teachings of the Bible. In fact, what they taught is closer to the actual Bible than the Bible you now use.

Well, I can feel myself start to move into reaction here. The Bible says it is the unalterable word of God, and you are saying it has been altered?

Do you not know this to be the case?

Yeah, but for some reason I don't want to let that one go.

Then work through it. You may help others release their conditioned thought as well.

Okay. Then I guess it's time to do a little research and move on to... Chapter 2?

Take it away.

Chapter 2

The Bible, For Instance

The history of religion and myth is all fairly simple to understand in terms of how it all came about.

I know a bit of classic Greek Literature, and I'm incredibly up on my history of the Bible having been raised in a very strict Christian home.

The Bible is a wonderful example of how and why religion forms, as well as how it changes and can be manipulated. You had something to say about this topic?

As a matter of fact, I do. In researching this material, I was a bit shocked to discover that none of the original books of the Bible are in existence today. What I mean by that is that the original Hebrew, Aramaic, and Latin texts have been destroyed. The earliest books that we have are written in Greek – which makes sense, as the most widely used language in the Mediterranean circa the fourth century was Greek (thank you Alexander the Great). From this time period, we have roughly 5,600 manuscripts of the New Testament. Out of these, there are over 200,000 "alleged" variants between these documents and the Bible we use today (included in that number are variations among the early works themselves and variations between the early works and our current Bible).

Do you wish to explain these variants, or should we?

I'd like to take a stab at it if you don't mind. I kind of enjoy the history. I think it's neat.

Then by all means, continue.

Well, one of the main reasons there are so many variants between the texts are because of the ways the earliest documents were translated. Keep in mind that all of the translations were done by hand, and not only does hand writing come into play, but so does language. Think about the English language. How many words have more than one meaning? It gets even more confusing when you look at Greek and all the root words in Latin. So, these books were copied with the unconscious bias of the individuals' own backgrounds – which included their socialization with regard to religion.

The earliest surviving copies of the New Testament (again, not in their original language, but in Greek) date back to around 125 AD (thank you google). The earliest surviving translation of Greek we have is from 180 AD. So, we actually have a book that is older than the earliest known translation of the language. I point that out because language evolves and around this time, the Bible began popping up in Latin, Coptic, and Syrian (thank you freshman year Bib lit!). In 300AD, the Coptic version (Coptic being a later version of the Egyptian language) was translated into the four dialects spoken in Egypt at the time. This will all be really important later on, so just kind of keep it in the back of your heads.

You are speaking to the reader?

Yeah. I know it's kind of like "Ugh. Get to the point already," but this will all come back into play later on.

So you think.

That was cryptic.

Are you finished.

Not even close.

In 323 AD, Constantine made Christianity the official religion of Rome. Shortly thereafter, the church held several Councils to decide their official positions. Topics which were debated in these Councils included the virgin birth, infant baptism, the marriage of priests, the Holy Spirit (the introduction of the "trinity" concept), and the divinity of Jesus.

Then, in 359AD, the Catholic Church began putting together what we know as the current Bible. They had a lot to sift through. Out of 200 proposed chapters – which at one time had all been viewed as part of the unchangeable word of God – the church took 46 books and created the Old Testament, and they took 27 for the New Testament. Now, some of you may think those numbers are off because your Bible only has 39 books in the Old Testament. Well, you've got to remember that whatever denomination you are, your beliefs sprang off from the Catholic church of the fourth Century. During the Protestant reformation, books were dropped.

I mentioned the 200,000 variants. In a Coptic Bible dated 350 A.D., the book of Mark ends with Chapter 16 verse 18. Today's version of The King James Bible has two additional verses and ends with a verse that did not exist in the original manuscript. Many changes, such as this, don't affect the message that much. Some of the alterations are simple omissions of a word or a misspelling, but some bring about significant changes in Christian doctrine.

For example, the concept of the Trinity (God as the Father, the Son and the Holy Spirit) does not appear in any copy of the book of John until the fifth century. In the original manuscripts, 1 John 5: 7-8 reads, "For there are three that testify: the spirit, *the water and the blood; and the three are in agreement." Today's version of the King James Bible reads, "<u>For there are three that bear record in heaven, the Father, the Word and the Holy Ghost; and these three are one. And there are three that bear witness in earth, the spirit, and the water, and the blood; and these three agree in one.</u>"*

The underlined verses above are not found in any original version of the New Testament – Greek or Latin. These words don't begin to appear until almost a hundred years after the divinity of Jesus was established by the church in the fourth Century. (As an interesting note from Wikipedia, when the first printed copy of the Greek New Testament was printed in 1514 by Saint Erasmus, it did not contain the added verses or any mention of the term "Trinity.")

That's quite a lot of research.

Oh, I've got more.

In the 1490's, Thomas Linacre, the personal physician of King Henry VIII and contemporary of Sir Thomas Moore, set out to compare a Greek version of the Bible to the Latin Vulgate. Of his comparison he wrote, "Either this is not the Gospel....or we are not Christians."

29

In 1516, Erasmus, another of Linacre's contemporaries had the Greek and Latin texts printed parallel to each other. In 1522, a version was published that contained the Aramaic, Hebrew, Greek and Latin texts all printed side by side. This version was used by William Tyndale in his English translations of both the New and Old Testaments in 1526 and 1530, respectively. Tyndale's Bible was the first time the text appeared translated in the English language.

In 1534, King Henry VIII formed the Church of England and split with the Catholic Church. Tyndale's Bible was used by the Church until around 1609. In 1603, James the first became King of England and Head of its church. In 1604, he appointed a group of linguists and biblical scholars to take another crack at translating the Greek and Hebrew into English. The task took five years, and the final product was dedicated to the King (earning its title as the King James Version).

Can we speak now?

Almost. We still have a few hundred years to plow through.

The final printing of the first King James Bible was completed in 1611, yet over the next few years, errors were discovered and corrections were needed. More than a century later, in 1727, the

King's printer issued an edition with several thousand errors in the Old Testament corrected. By 1769, extensive revision had been made and almost 35,000 notes added. In 1873, the American Bible Society studied six different editions of the King James Bible. They found more than 24,000 variants in just the six editions they examined.

Thomas Jefferson took it upon himself to learn Greek and compare the Greek manuscripts of the Bible with the King James Version. He was so disappointed with the results that he wrote his own English version of the Bible, which later became known as the Jeffersonian Bible.

In 1872 a team of English and American scholars began work on yet another interpretation of the Bible. The "Revised Version" New Testament was published in 1881 with the Old Testament appearing in 1885. In 1901, the agreement between the British and the American teams expired, and the "Revised Version, Standard American Edition" was born. In 1928, the body that would later become the National Council of Churches acquired the copy write. By 1952, this version had become widely popular in seminaries and had garnered the nickname "The Standard Bible."

The last of the translations (we're almost through, I promise) came as a reaction to the

31

"Revised Version." Evangelical Protestants took exception to certain texts regarding Mary's virginity as well as the presentation of other Old Testament doctrines. In 1973, the New York Bible Society released the NIV New Testament. The full Bible was released in 1978 and was revised again in 1984.

So, there you go. That's a lot of historically authenticated altering for an unalterable and unaltered document.

Indeed. Now do us all a favor and claim "I am Self Love" around everything you have just said. You've stirred up quite a bit of energy there.

Sorry. I am Self-Love.

Now, love yourself enough not to apologize (Laughter).

You haven't done anything wrong. We're merely pointing out that you stirred up energies within your own creation that you yourself need to balance, bring together, change, alter, or let go of.

Ah. Well, thank you... So, I'm almost done.

I want to squeeze in that along the way the Gnostic Gospels were buried (and then recovered), and hell and purgatory were added to the cannon. The lake of fire <u>does</u> appear several times in John, yet it appears in reference to the "second death"

and is used metaphorically. John's lake of fire –
while interpreted the same in all English versions of
the Bible – is not the same place that has been
interpreted as "hell" in other parts of the English
Bible. The original appearances of what was later
translated into "hell" are Sheol – which literally
translates into "shallow grave" and Gehana –
which was a literal geographical location just
outside of the city where the dead were burned. I
bring that up because as these places were
introduced, it then became possible for a time to buy
your way out of both. Around this time, the earth
was pronounced flat, and Christmas took the place
of the Pagan holiday celebrating the birth of Horus
(an Egyptian deity who was believed to have been
the born of a virgin son of God who was crucified,
rose from the dead, and then ascended into heaven).

And how can you love this energy – which is you
- when you judge it so harshly?

Yeah. I did get a bit carried away there. I felt
that. I think it's just because I was raised to believe
in a God who kind of hated me. The idea of hell still
pushes my buttons, I guess.

Do you not know by now that if something
"pushes your buttons" it's because you're in reaction
to something? What are you holding in your own

story that you haven't let go of that plugs you into judgment?

I guess it's the part I just said.

So can you let that go?

I am Self-Love.

We would suggest expanding your consciousness so that you can know love and release this on behalf of all of your energy – on behalf of all consciousness. For if God hates you, then *you* hate you, and you hate all that is God – which is all that is. If you are still holding that, how can you truly release anything? You cannot and will not because you will punish yourself by hanging on to your baggage and continue to be the martyr of your own creation – thus never fully creating from a new place. Love yourself and release yourself from these thoughts. Is that not the true message of Christ? Did he not come to show the way to union with the Father – the Creator of all life that *is* all life - that we all may be in union and harmony with Divine Love?

Yes.

Good. Now that you have spent your energy studying the church and the origin of your doctrines, are you ready to move beyond? Are you ready to look at these documents and institutions for what they are?

34

Yes, and what are they?

As you have just passionately shown by exposing your own judgments and thoughts, they are markers of consciousness and understanding. That is all.

You're going to have to explain that one. You're saying the Bible itself is a consciousness marker, or that all of these periods of time were markations of consciousness?

Indeed; we are saying both. For the book itself is man's way of knowing more about who and where he is as well as from where he comes (where he still is) and where he will return. We have explained to you previously in *Love, Life, God* that consciousness is all that is. Everything exists in the moment of now. All possibilities are potential, and all potential is explored: be it in this environment – that which you recognize as your physical time and space location - or any "other."

What we are saying with regard to the consciousness is that throughout history, man's perspective of who he is has evolved. In the beginning, (and by that we mean that which you think of as the beginning), man separated from God when he became consciously aware of himself as separate. Nothing changed in the realm of physical matter, only perception.

So you're saying that just as Adam walked with God in the garden, I walk with God now?

You walk as God *with* God. In terms of the story, man knew God as he knew himself, for the two were the same. When man "ate the fruit" of consciousness, he became aware of himself through the eyes of his ego. He saw himself as separate. We are saying "he" here, and the same holds true for the female. To move even beyond the physical, the male and the female did not separate until they became aware of themselves as individual aspects.

Okay, huh? Is that like saying God has male and female qualities?

A better way to say what you have said would be, "males and females have the qualities of God." What you think of as male and female qualities are qualities of God – of the All. Within the One, there is no "other." Male and female are the same.

So why do we exist on this plane as male and female?

To learn about your Self, you may seek to form in many different ways. What you term female energy can be stronger in a male than in a female, yet that does not make the male any less of a male. The same holds true for a female. Gender is not necessarily related to the expansion of the male or female energy. You are here to simply expand, and gender is but one ingredient you choose when creating that which you will call your self. Remember what we said in our first book, you exist as an individualized expression simultaneously in an infinite amount of "places," all of which are occurring in the ever-expansive moment of now. You may be experiencing life as you are focusing on it here as a male while experiencing a simultaneous life as a female. In fact, if we are to truly address this idea or notion of gender, you are existing as other species which defy gender explanations. How far do you wish to expand? The answer to this question will determine the allowance of your own knowingness.

Well I'd like to stick to this plane, at least for now.

Very well. The balance between the sexes is a reflection of the balance within your individualized selves. If you seek to damage a woman, you seek to reject or do harm to that part of yourself you view as "woman." The same applies in the reverse. All outer imbalance is reflective of inner discord.

The One Energy – of which you are - is All; it is All there is. Within this isness, there exists no separation. That which you call God is no more male than female. It is no more one thing than another. Do you know the phrase "split a piece of wood and there I Am?"

Yes. I believe that is from the book of Thomas.

Indeed. Do you know why it is worded this way? In fact it is worded the same way in which the words of Christ were recalled; do you know why?

You mean, "I Am?"

Yes. As we have said, the Bible was laid out by man – man wishing to know more from whom he is, yet also <u>not</u> wanting to know. The collective of your consciousness on this plane is a simple thing: it is the totality of you. It has not easily been grasped by your mind up to this point the true nature of "all are one." As we will discuss, man channeled that which he called God, yet he did not realize it was his own inner voice calling out. Some embraced the voice; some fell upon their faces and worshipped it. Others imposed their own fears and limited concepts upon it. Again, this is not wrong in any means. It is simply the evolution of your mind as a whole. To prove or disprove anything is not the point. For as we have said, there is no place of "there" to reach. There is no "higher" state to attain. There is simply expansion, and within this great book – as well as all other great books - man laid out his true nature. Our function here is to simply love and provide – as you have asked – a "new" perspective. Yet, you will see there is nothing "new" about it. The energy has been there all along. You simply couldn't be given until you asked, and you couldn't find until you truly chose to seek.

Chapter 3

The Great I Am and the Isness of All

It is interesting, in many respects, that most people think of God as an entity outside or beyond their being. We say interesting, not because it is an abnormal thing, but rather it's interesting with respect to your thoughts about God, and your relationship to your universe according to these beliefs.

Why is that interesting?

It's interesting because many still hold "God" as a sovereign being, and indeed, God is sovereign – for all of creation is given according to their vibration. For example, if your vibrations are the totality of conflicting belief systems or conflicting thoughts about money, you will continue to manifest according to those beliefs or vibrations. If you are the totality of love, love will come forth and be given. So, we're not talking of God as the Creative Force of all or the Energy of Everything, we are talking about God as an idea, and with this idea comes the notion that "It is out of my hands."

Now, bear with us. We feel you wanting to interject, but hold off. We do know where this is going.

Take the construct of the traditional idea of God: People worship, fear, praise, ask, and act all in the name of this idea. God must be pleased – and this is where we break off into potentiality as far as subject. For some, they only feel good knowing they are pleasing to God. For others, God must be pleased to avoid horrible suffering in this life or the next. Others sacrifice themselves for God or endure a lifetime of self-denial – which we find to be the ultimate paradox, for how could God deny itself that which it is? Only a sovereign God would allow itself such total freedom and Love.

You're saying that self-sacrifice requires love?

Indeed. For God so loved the world… You see this idea within the collective has been around for thousands of years. "God loves us so much, that He sacrificed his own Son." In reality, we are all that Son. How much love would have to exist for sacrifice to be allowed? You see, The One Energy is pure Source – only through direction is it defined. Source does not judge anything, it simply says, "I love you; Yes." You see, and we're moving very quickly here, but every single individualized expression of Source energy creates its own life – its own field, its own belief system, etc. The One Energy just says, "To my beloved, you may have whatever you call forth."

In other words, The One Energy – God – is not really caught up in our drama because God is never worried about anything.

Yes, that is what we are saying. In previous conversations documented in *Love, Life, God: The Journey of Creation* , we discussed with you the structure of your universe and how thoughts correspond to the physical world and how everything is really no thing and every thing and together and separate all at the same time. With that understanding, you can clearly see that the drama is only perceived by the human mind – which again – is a function of the ego, which simply serves as the vehicle for this individualized experience to come into being. God – NOT the IDEA of God – but God as Pure Source Energy, has nothing to worry about – and you ARE that Energy.

I think I said something like that to someone today at lunch. We were talking about life and I said, "The truth is man, you're already there. All of this is just the story of how it happened." Is that kind of what we're talking about?

We would add the understanding that there is no there separate from here.

That's what I meant.

Then indeed, you were correct. At your highest level, you know that none of the things that go on in your life are really THAT dramatic. Yes, you believe you must make money. You believe you must protect and nourish your children. Why? In one hundred years, what will that matter? What about five hundred or a thousand? What you really want is a feeling. You want to feel the joy and love that you are. So you see, after thousands upon thousands of years, the collective mind has said "enough!" You as an individualized expression of Source have said "Enough!" And again, all of these years, all of this time, all of these moments are happening simultaneously. They are available to be experienced at any time – even within your own moment of now.

What do you mean?

Going back to our clock metaphor from *Love, Life, God*, you know that all time, space, dimensions, etc. exists in the moment of now. It's only your perception and choice to physically manifest into this point that puts you in this particular time and space. So, within the One Energy, All that ever will be, is. There is no past, present, or future.

So it really is One Big Ride?

One Big Love. The Ride – as you call it – is what many people are choosing to no longer experience.

44

There is a movement back to the Oneness of God. This is why religion was birthed in the first place. Even the religions which required the taking of life were upheld by the desire to connect with the divine – whether through pleasure or pain. All religion – and we want you to really GET this – *__All__* religion serves God because it represents the desire for Him. And please explain that "Him" is your interpretation for what we show to be God. We communicate in energy, so for your interpretation to be masculine simply shows where the Energy is with relation to its own story of male and female identification.

Is that important?

Only if you create it as such (laughter).

Honestly, I think maybe I am creating it to be important because I still hold this charge around the word God. If someone says Source or Energy, I feel like it is this loving, neutral thing, but I immediately associate the word God with a patriarchal male figure.

…And oh, to be in a female body.

Wow. Yeah. I guess in my head, God is made in my image.

And you are made in the image of God, but that message was simply misunderstood - for what are you? You are not gender. You are not white, black,

45

brown, red, or blue. You are you. God is all things to all people because God is all things and God *is* all people. It is only when God becomes an outside Source that the fighting begins. If God is outside, how do I get to God? How do I please God? What must I do to get God to do things for me? You see these are all questions that arise from the belief that God is separate. We have titled this chapter, "The Great I AM and the Isness of All" for a reason. We want to explain to you something many people don't grasp – including yourself, which we say lovingly. If you fully knew it, you would exemplify it, and you would not occasionally waver in any deed or thought.

Well, and I say this lovingly, isn't it human to sometimes wonder about decisions and the effects of our actions?

No. It is the story you have ascribed to your own humanity. For you see, as the story goes, and you may cite the exact passage if you wish, but a man went up a mountain – because there were no freeways at that time –

Did you just make a joke?

Yes. Lighten up (laughter).

You know the story. The man you know as Moses was given a message by God. Moses was

46

then given specific instructions – which of course came from him (Moses) via his own higher connection to The One – and was brought about by the desire of the people to connect to the divine. Moses asked Source, "who shall I tell them sent me?" Source replied, "I AM." Now, the concept here is eternal. It was even recorded as such in the words that followed. As the story goes, God said, "This is to be my monument for all generations." Now, as you know, Moses didn't speak the language you speak, therefore, a different name was given. Just as you translated our energy of Source into the word "Him," so Moses translated what roughly amounts to "It is I Who are you," I Am THAT I Am.

Wow. I'm sorry, I know that's the second "wow" moment this chapter for me, but... WOW! "It is I Who are You!?"

And the message was carried down, yet the meaning was understood only by a few. Remember, in those times, idol worship was prevalent, just as it is today.

What do you mean "just as it is today?" Not too many people worship idols.

Oh but they do.

If you ask your car to bring you money, will it?

Only if I sell it.

Therefore that car has no real power, does it?

No. It can get me places though.

But you see what we mean. You know how a car operates, and you know how a car is made, but if you were to take that car to the time of Moses, it would be seen as something to be worshipped. It would seemingly have the power to move people at high speeds, shield them from the elements, run down walls, or cause great harm. You wouldn't worship a car because your mind understands what a car is. You wouldn't acknowledge a car as a great creative force in your life. It's simply a tool you use to drive to the places you want to go. If you didn't have a car, you would take the bus, or walk, or find some other way to get wherever you wanted to go – all according to your vibrations – your spectral output.

Spectral output?

You know from our previous conversations that everything is energy. Think of your world as a giant canvas, only instead of paint and color, it is comprised of music, of frequency, of light. Your spectral output is the total creation – the totality of your musical resonance – vibrating as all of creation as you create it.

So, my "spectral output" is basically my beliefs in action? It is the finished product?

In so much as anything is ever finished. It is a continual work in progress – ever growing and changing – but yes; it is what you experience as the whole of your creation.

How then does my spectral output relate back to idol worship and the car?

Excellent question. The commandment not to have any other Gods really comes from the desire to know your own connection to Source – to know <u>Thy Self</u>. In other words, who are you?

What do you mean?

It's not a trick question. What are you?

I am Source Energy.

Yes, and you get that to a point. What we would like to show you is where you fall out of that knowing - the point where you stop knowing thy Self. The minute you stop knowing thy Self as the creator of all, you have placed another God before you.

In your life right now, and we know this is hard for you, so play along, in your life right now, what is going on?

Well, we've finished our first book , and now we've moved on to book number two.

Yes, and how is that going?

Well, the writing is coming along fine. I've been a little hesitant to begin this book...

...Even though the information has been coming in.

Yes. The information has been coming in. In fact, Several times, I've even ignored you and pretended like I didn't understand you. The messages kept coming in varying ways, and you've finally gotten me back to the computer to write about some of the things we've been discussing.

Yes, but what is going on with the first book?

Well, I've submitted it to a few literary agents, and right now I'm working with an editor – who, by the way, I don't know how I'm going to pay.

Do you really want to claim that?

No.

You know you will be provided for once you move out of your way. What we would like to show is how you have gotten in your way to begin with – how you've impeded your flow by worshipping a false god.

Excuse me? I'm worshipping a false god?

Absolutely. What have you made your main focus these last three months?

Publishing my book.

Indeed. And is your book published?

No.

And how does that make you feel?

Well, I'm not thrilled. I guess you could say I occasionally get a little pissy about it. I've got this great book, we've been working with all kinds of people, touching lives, and I feel like I have nothing to show for it.

Nothing to show? A woman and her husband – people you had not seen in years - recently visited you in the night, did they not?

Yes. I had a sort of waking dream where her husband brought her to me and said "I just need for her to tell me its okay to go."

And literally, two days later, you saw this woman, right?

Yes. She came to watch my friend and co-author of The Big E – Everything is Energy, Dee Wallace, give a speech.

51

And you went up and hugged her and didn't even bother to mention the dream, did you?

No, I waited until after she had spoken to Dee, then I pulled Dee aside and told her instead.

And what happened?

She grabbed me by the arm, chased the woman down, and had me tell her what I experienced.

And what was the woman's reaction?

Her eyes welled up with tears. She told me that two nights prior, the same night I had my dream, she had been awakened by her husband who was talking in his sleep. All she heard him say was "I need for her to tell me." She didn't know what he needed, and she even woke him up to ask him what he was dreaming about, but he didn't know. She then looked at me, and through tears began to tell me that he had cancer and was dying.

And you felt love, right? You felt an overwhelming sense of just how connected everyone truly is. You touched her and gave her peace, yet you feel like you have nothing to show?

Well, I feel really bad about it when you put it like that. I live for those moments. I have them all the time.

Yes, but you don't fully allow yourself to experience them.

What do you mean?

You just gloss on by. To you, these things are "normal," so you shut out the connection and the love because "normal" has no value. Money, however, has value. Money is your God.

What?

Why has publishing your book been so important? You enjoyed writing it, didn't you?

Yes. Absolutely. It was one of the best experiences of my life.

Yet, does it have value to you right now?

The book, or the experience?

They are the same.

...No. I guess not.

Then you see how your creation is at work even now. You've made selling your book into your God. You have made it a reflection of your worth and who you are. You have said, "In order to know its value, I need someone to buy it. I need someone to give me money. I need people to want it." In doing that, you have limited your Self in so many ways. You have prevented yourself from having the experience of totally immersing yourself in what you know. You've pulled back and said, "I know this, but…" And any time you throw in a "but," you cancel out whatever came before it.

How though have I made my book God?

It has become the thing that has power over you. It has power over your finances. It has power over your mood. It has power over your reputation and self worth. It has this power because you have given this power to it. Take that power back. We're talking not just to you. We're using you as an example, but the same can be said to almost everyone reading these words. It is time to take your power back from money.

Yes, I want to. How?

Set it free. Remember, love is. There are no conditions. You have energetically made a vow to love your creation only when it brings you money. It has brought you reasons to meet new people, share your Self, teach, and do the things you love, yet you've not set it free – you've not set yourself free, and thus are committing idolatry. You are ascribing a power to the sale of your book: "If I sell this book, I will be happy. I will be rich. I will be good enough. I will be…" Fill in the blank. Those "ifs" have kept you from experiencing the joy of the process you have chosen to undertake. Many readers have done the same: with relationships, with jobs, with their children, etc.

Your book doesn't bring you money, just as a car doesn't bring you money. It's a vehicle, just as all energy is a vehicle, and it must be driven, just as you must climb into your role of creator and create – drive your energy to the destination to which you wish to arrive. Do you see how you have had many gods BEFORE God – before You?

Wow. Yes. When you start to break it down like that, I can see numerous places in my life where I've made other things my God. I've made my agents God. They've become the means by which I get a job or at the very least they are the people who have to get me in the door.

And in reality, you do those things. You may attract certain people to fulfill tasks, but it's all done by you.

I've made other things my God too.

Yes. You've become so caught up in the illusion lately – so caught up in not knowing Thy Self as you truly are - that you've become fearful.

Very much so.

And do you know what you fear? You fear Knowing your Self, because in knowing who you are, you are also knowing who you are not. You are not all of those stories you held about yourself, and that scares you. It makes you feel unsafe.

I didn't consciously realize that's what was going on, but I've been having panic attacks again recently. The attacks stopped several years ago, and I've been medication free for years. Then, one day, wham!

Oh no. It was not one day. Your resonance changed slowly but surely. Certain events simply served to show you places in your life that you had previously not been willing to go. Physically, you simply became aware that there were still some notes in the overall symphony that were a little flat.

Haha. I just started to feel myself feeling bad.

Indeed. You started to give yourself the gift of victimization – another God you worship. When you can be a victim, you can be saved, and you can express emotion. You've been having anxiety because you've been judging your emotion and not allowing yourself to be as you are. As we mentioned in book one, if you stub your toe, it might sting at first. You might whence. You might even curse your toe or whatever you stubbed it on. Yet, after a few seconds of expression, you would more than likely move on and forget about your toe. You would make a mental note to be careful or to pay more attention

56

next time, and you would let the energy go. Emotionally, you have stubbed your Self, only you've not let it go. You've attempted to suck it up because you've confused walking your talk with being a robot. You basically had no other way to get your attention than to start physically experiencing what you feel as panic – the energy was there and it simply found a way to manifest. You plug in very fast to your body, and you pay attention. We could scream and yell at you all day (and some days we do), and you ignore us. You ignore what you know; you ignore what you feel emotionally. You detach, but when you "feel" in the physical sense that something is wrong, boy do you stop and take note. In this way, you also worship illness. It is something that governs you instead of something you govern. And again, we are using you as an example, but we really mean the broader "you" that is humanity.

Illness is simply a symptom, an experience, yet you view it as some great entity outside of your creation. In reality, it is simply a way for You to get your attention. It's an expression of energy, pure and simple. You create and command all energy. It just frightens you to be fully present. These episodes are not attacks. They are creations, and they are yours. You don't need to create them any longer. Yet, if an "episode" is created, experience it. Dive in and be

57

with it. Face the fear – whatever it may be - and stand firm in your presence.

Whoa. I didn't really expect it to get all personal.

Yes you did. That's why you haven't come in to write even though you've known the gist of this chapter for months now. You didn't want to look at the things in your life that you had made into God. Parts of you still don't.

You see, the most basic definition of God is "creator." So, who and what is God in your life? We'd like to take a moment here as well to point out to the reader that the belief or idea of "giving myself up" or "giving up everything" is simply another aspect of creation that has been given God status.

Explain that and how it ties in, will you?

Certainly. First, let's balance everything we've discussed by claiming I Am Self Love.

I AM Self Love!

Indeed. Now, if the belief is held with regard to Spiritual growth that: "I will give up everything and do whatever it takes to know my oneness with Source," you will worship lack. Inherent in that belief is another belief that says, "Source requires me to give up the things that I want in order to know who and what I am. What I am is creation itself,

58

therefore in order to know it I will give up knowing it."

You're saying that if I believe I have to "take up my cross" and follow God, I am serving my own smallness?

That is one way of looking at it, yes. You are saying, "I will sacrifice myself and my own wants for God, because that is what God wants." Yet, you are the God who wants it. If such a belief is present, it's there for a reason; yet, if you are reading these words, we would suggest that you – much like most of consciousness – are ready to give up that story and discover that heaven truly lies within.

And knowing that leads to the creation of heaven as a physically attainable state?

Indeed. Again, as above, so below; as within, so without. All we are saying is, know that you don't have to give up anything other than limitation. You don't have to suffer in this existence unless you've made suffering a God. It all depends on your own limitations around the story of creation. Who and what are you allowing to create your life? For you, the image of who you should be (and for that matter, who you should be with), how your life should look, what your family and friends will think, and what projects you should be working on, are all things that you allow to hold you back and create for you.

Your image of how life "should" look is inflexible, and in that inflexibility, you are sacrificing your own limitless creative ability. You are fighting the very things you wish to create because you are not allowing You to create. You are putting that responsibility on things, on people, even on us. We are you. Those things are you. But you have to realize and consciously know that You are the creative force. You are driving the car. The car isn't driving you.

You just stopped writing but came right back, why?

I started thinking about working. Wow. I have a hard time typing "I work as a voice over actor."

Why do you think that is?

Because I haven't really made much of a living this year.

And you realize that's because you consciously made something else your God.

Yes.

But you had a realization that brought you back to the computer. What was it?

I realized that I'd made "NOT making work my God," into my God. In doing so, I was directing my

energy NOT to bring me work. I still only kind of
understand, but I know this is big.

Indeed it is. It's a "whopper" as you might say.
You knew that work was not your god, so you set
out to prove this to yourself by experiencing a world
in which work didn't create your income. You made
your parents and their money God, and with that,
you made their belief systems your God because you
had to bend to their will in order to keep a roof over
your head – at least that was your perception. Then,
you began to desire work. You chose a field that was
fun and exciting and where the payoff was
enormous. You made close to six figures for two or
three days of work, and guess what? You enjoyed it
– and then you made money your God. You set out
once again to prove that work was not your God, so
you stopped working. Now, the lack of work has
brought forth this desire in you to work, but it has
also caused you to suffer in the self worth
department – all though we would like to say that
you've done a pretty nice job of only enjoying the
pity on a surface level only.

Gee… thanks?

What we mean by that is that you're aware that
you're playing this game and it's become harder for
you to buy into your own drama. But what you've
done is made NOT working your God – because

only by not working can you know you create. This is your version of bearing a cross. You haven't known it was never about the work – it was always about you. You worked when you knew you could create work. Do you follow?

Yes. You're saying that I worked because of me, not because of my agents or because of the advertisers, or anything else.

And we're also saying it wasn't NOT because of them. They are all reflections of you. THAT is what you have separated. You have said, "well, if I work, work will be my god," instead of, "I provide, and I am using this avenue of creation to explore who I am, and I will create my life in this manner." You have worked and worshipped your work. You have then sent yourself the message that "this is not god," but you've thrown the baby out with the bath water.

It's like this: if you're sick but will allow your body to heal through medicine, take the medicine.

Isn't that making the medicine God?

No, and that's where you get hung up. It's simply a means created by you. It was brought into your awareness *by* you *for* you. It's as your friend once said, "God is just as much a carrot as God is chemotherapy." You eat every day, yet you don't feel like food is your God do you?

...well, I love me some burgers, but no. I don't think of food as having creative authority in my life.

And so it is with medicine. So it is with work. So it is with relationships. So it is with every thing and every one.

This brings up an interesting energy in you. Why do you feel that money has power over you, yet food doesn't? If you starve, will your body not physically die?

Yeah, but I don't really worry about food. However, I do stress about what I'm doing for a living.

Would you like to know why?

Yes.

Because you have ascribed a value to work that is outside of yourself. Food you take for granted – it's always there - but work is "important." You know what else is "important?"

...God.

Exactly. So we would suggest claiming Self-Love around all of the things in your life that you have separated from God – put before God – so that everything can be made one, and the power – the importance – lies within.

I Am Self-Love.

And so it is. Now we'd like to discuss the "isness" and more of the "I am."

Okay; go.

That which is termed "isness" is the being that is all things. It's both ever changing and static at the same time. Within the realm of the One, lies all possibility; this much you know. What escapes you at this moment is that within that realm also lies the potentiality – the possibility – for all things to occur.

As all things occur, no thing occurs.

Okay. That sounds like another one of those "Buddha on the mountain top" type sayings that doesn't really mean anything.

Indeed it will mean as much as you allow it to mean.

Well, my brain looks at that and says, "Okay. So, everything is. It just is... whether it is or not"

Not "It JUST is." You create, and it is. You create! Physically manifesting a situation or occurrence in this time space reality is no more of a creation than not manifesting that particular thing.

Okay, so I create, and it is, but within the isness, the possibility exists for every single expression or occurrence to manifest... be they known or unknown to me on the conscious level, right?

Yes. And to look at creation as simply an act that calls something forth is to limit creation. Creation is all things. You think of creation as occurring only when something is brought forth, but in every single moment, you are being brought forth. You are always creating, whether you consciously recognize (re-cognize) that you are creating everything. And everything may be known on the conscious level. That is one of the potentials you are not focusing on at the moment. If you could focus on that not just as potential, but as fact, your mood would greatly improve.

What you are doing now is coming at us from your head and not your heart. Your head tells you that everything is possible, yet you don't believe it's <u>probable</u>, and this must change in order for you to grow into the role you've chosen to grow into. You must be able not just to create, but to receive your creation.

I guess that's why you're here.

That is why YOU are here.

Okay. So, I am Self-love. I choose to see not just potential around me, but to actualize that potential and see – to know – possibility and probability everywhere. I choose to know what I Am and that I Am and create the life I want to experience and express myself as I Am – and love myself as I Am.

65

Probability to you means problem. Are you aware of that consciously?

Well, no… but I can feel the truth there.

Look at it this way: probability is nothing more than the percentage of your allowance. How much would you like to give yourself? That's all probability is. If you have a problem freely giving to yourself or freely receiving from yourself on any level, now would be the time to address that.

I am divine love. I am Self love.

Why did I do that? Why did I say divine love and Self Love? Come to think of it, why did I capitalize Self but not divine?

Do you really need to ask? What an interesting chapter. You've exalted your Self above the divine. You have created and separated concepts of self and god, and then in your attempt to get back together, you've made the self greater – which in this case limits Source because you are vibrationally saying "I Am divine," yet you're holding a definition of divine as something outside, and your self – the you that is aware that it's separating – is having an internal struggle. On the one hand, it's saying "I am all things and therefore I am God" – capital G – All That Is, but on the other hand, it's saying "in order to be God" – capital G – All That Is – "there must be

A God" – capital G in the sense of One God outside of Self – "and I am NOT THAT God."

Holy shit.

Yes. And no. It's wholly shit (laughter).

You are wholly focused on this dichotomy – thus *creating* the dichotomy of self and God. The dichotomy does not actually exist, except for when it does.

In other words, as I believe?

As you believe, as you perceive... same thing. You perceive anything based on or through the belief that created it. You think that perception is separate from belief, but it's not. Beliefs go beyond thought, you know. They go beyond the level of cellular or atomic. Beliefs can be etheric. They can be emotional...

Hold on. What is etheric?

As we use the term, it's used to demonstrate "space" between. For example, you think of solid matter as solid, yet it's not. It's comprised of space. There is also space in the way that you think of separation between objects or bodies. This space is not empty. So, "etheric" accounts for the space that is not space. It is all levels of belief that lies between all levels of matter, and vice versa.

So, beliefs are not just your thoughts – all though you know the phrase "a belief is a thought that is thought over and over again?" On some level, you could have a thought because of a belief held somewhere in your energy. The definition given above ascribes consciousness to beliefs, but everything is consciousness – not just your mind. Remember from book one, we told you how vibrations are made up of frequencies and frequencies are made up of vibrations, just like a harp chord may be one chord made up of many chords. Well, you think of beliefs as ideas or values held in the mind, and in fact, this is not correct.

Well, let's move on to the next chapter and see if we can't head down this rabbit hole a little further.

Get ready to dive in, hatter.

Chapter 4

The Body of Christ

You don't like our title?

It seems a little out of place and almost sacrilegious to me.

Direct your own consciousness to suspend your beliefs about religion while we explore this topic. These beliefs are yours, and they'll do as you instruct them, but know that you'll only follow a direct command. If you tell yourself to do something, yet you don't actually wish your self to follow through, the self will respond accordingly. You can't lie to your Self, ever. "Thou shalt not lie," remember? A better way to say this would be, "there is no such thing as a lie."

Huh?

You may deceive, but you deceive in words or deed only. There has to be a thought in motion behind the word or deed, and behind that, an intention. The energy is clear as far as the objective. Do you understand?

I understand. I'm not sure I agree, but I understand.

That hit a nerve, eh? Would you like to move beyond that and expand? Remember, it's always okay to say "no." Don't judge yourself for whatever answer you choose to give. Either is fine.

Well, yes, I'd like to move on from that.

Then simply do so. It really is that easy.

All right. So, in "reality" – you like what I did there? I put reality in quotes. I'm learning...

Indeed.

In "reality" there is no such thing as a lie because the energy just manifests what is directed, right?

Mostly. Your words are correct, but your energy is not yet clear. Would you direct clarity and claim knowing?

I am Self-Love. I know All That Is.

Wow. I just got the shivers.

Because you truly chose to let go, and everything in your field quickly adjusted.

Okay, so this chapter is called "The Body of Christ." Why?

Because we want to use a metaphor you're familiar with to illustrate the principals of quantum being-ness.

70

Quantum being-ness?

Yes. We've discussed isness and being-ness, and we want to relate that to All That Is – we would say beyond the body, but nothing is beyond the body. To your mind, the Universe still exists outside of you, and what we wish to show you is that it really exists everywhere. You are all things and all things are you. The Universe out there (the Universe you term as outside of your physical expression) is really the same Universe as "inside."

"The Kingdom of heaven is within?" "As above, so below?" "Split a piece of wood and there I Am?"

I get it; I get it.

To some extent, yes. We'd like to go further.

At the close of chapter three, we were discussing beliefs and the mind. Most people think of the mind as a function of the brain or as a function of consciousness. The latter is more correct, all though it is still limited in large part by what the mass consciousness views as "consciousness."

Whoa whoa whoa. The mass consciousness AND consciousness?

Good for you. You caught that.

Wouldn't those two things be the same thing?

Do you really want to go down this path?

Yes. Yes, I do.

We love it when you go with the flow.

All right, we talked a little bit about mass consciousness and it's relation to individual expression in the first book. Basically, the mass consciousness is whatever the singular consciousness projects as a total unit. Back to the harp, mass consciousness is the totality of all of the chords being played. Now, in this example, one chord can change the way the whole unit of sound is expressed, however, each chord is still a separate and unique chord unto itself.

Thus is the body of Christ. As you understand this metaphor, the body of Christ is what?

Well, the "body" of Christ is the total collection of Christ's followers.

Indeed. And what have we told you about that which you call Christ – which could also be termed Atman, Budha, Ra or "peanut butter" if you prefer. These are only words, but what is the energy they represent?

Union with God.

Indeed, Oneness with God. These words represent the wiping away of separation.

I'm sorry. I totally spaced out. I forgot what we were talking about.

It's all right. You've just had an experience of what we're talking about. Would you like to discuss the feeling?

It was like I totally left. Everything was gone, and then here I was, and everything was back. "Welcome home" someone just said. It's really strange, but I feel like there's a party going on over there.

There is. We're having a great time. It was nice of you to pop in and join us for a moment. (Laughter).

You just had an experience of Oneness.

I just had more shivers.

Yes, your vibration shifted because you just judged your experience and weren't sure how you felt about it. You were totally fine until you analyzed it and began to fear it. Could you tell you were moving out of joy and into fear?

I could. It was the strangest thing. Everything was so peaceful, but once I regained my bearings, it was like "Oh shit. What was that?"

That was the mind – not the mind in the broader sense, which we will discuss, but the mind of limitation. By the way, the mind of limitation is only there because you put it there. You could change that whenever you decided to. We're not saying that to judge, we just felt your question coming.

What does that mean?

The mind "in the broader sense" is the same thing as the body of Christ – which is really the body of everything and nothing. It is All That Is. It's all that we are, and it's all that you are. The limited mind is the mind you associate with your beliefs. However, neither is separate from that which you are.

We've spoken with you before in private about identity, and you know that there are many instances of people who've had some type of brain trauma or some such thing and they have literally forgotten how to read or how to speak. In some cases, they've forgotten who they were before their "injury." It's as if they were "born again" from a clean slate.

You're just not going to let the Christian metaphors go are, you.

"Hell" no. They are so appropriate because they are NOT metaphors. They've just been so limited. You see, being born again is not some symbolic act of taking the bread and drinking the wine, or even of accepting a savior. It is a literal process.

Well, is it a standard process?

Sure. It's Self-Love. You joked with your friend that the true recipe for knowing was trusting and allowing, but which part of you is doing those things?

I tend to think that...

That was a rhetorical question, but thank you for taking the bait. You "think," do you?

Uh-oh. Here we go.

Remember that wonderful phrase we mentioned in the beginning of book one, "You are the totality of all you have ever thought?"

Yes.

Well, now seems as good a time as any to let you in on a little secret. You don't just think with your thoughts.

Somebody in the heavens just cranked up Lionel Richie.

"Turn on Your Heart Light."

Ugh. That's gonna be stuck in my head all day.

Good. We hope it never leaves. You see, you know that thoughts create. But what you don't know is that feelings are the anchors that keep them in place.

Well, sure I do. If I feel good and I'm getting everything I want, there's nothing left to do. I'm doing it, right?

Wrong. There is always something to do. Humanity has this strange idea that heaven is an attainable yet static material state. There's nothing static about any of it. Heaven is always changing. Do you want to spend eternity lying in a hammock by the beach drinking mai tai's?

Actually, that doesn't sound so bad.

Okay. Done. Your heaven is now here. Hop into the hammock and start sipping away. Nice, huh?

Yeah.

Let's just hope you don't have to pee anytime soon.

Huh?

Or get hungry.

Oh, I get it.

Do you? True heaven is not static, it is the freedom to choose whatever you want and have it in that moment. There are no ties to it, no rules… just the experience you've asked for, and once you've had that experience, you're free to want and have another. It might be similar, it might even start out

76

the same, but the point is you're creating it as you go.

What does that have to do with my heart light?

The heart light is how it all works. You know the saying that you say over and over, "You can't get there from your mind?"

Yes.

What do you think that really means?

Oh, no. I'm not falling for that one again. I don't "think" it means anything. I know what it means. It means that you just have to let go and trust and get out of your head.

Right. Get out of your head, but not because being there is a bad thing. We'll use you as an example.

Oh boy.

No. You'll like this one.

So, you were thinking about what to do with regard to book one. Shortly after finishing the first book, you met an editor you absolutely loved, and you booked two commercial accounts that would take care of just about an entire years worth of bills as well as the editing fees. Does all of this sound correct so far?

Well, I actually leapt into writing this book right after finishing the first draft of the last one, but yeah, that's all correct. It was interesting though because I actually met the editor...

(Laughter) You stopped. You must know where this is going.

So, describe for the reader what happened next.

Well, I actually met the editor while he was in town working on another project for a friend of mine. For whatever reason, I'd chosen to drive to Malibu that morning (something I'd only done a few times before in all the years I'd lived in California). On the way back, I had a horrible panic attack. It just so happened that my friend lived just over the canyon road, and I stopped at her house to lie down and recover. I remember feeling sick for a few weeks after that.

That was a purging. You tend to do that.

I've noticed.

Look at the writing for a moment. You'll notice you said you were "sick," whereas we said you were "purging."

What's the difference?

You weren't sick. Yes, you felt nauseous and queasy, but it's important for you to get that you weren't sick. You were more well then, than you were just before. You were so well compared to how you had been, that you needed to close a gap in a relatively short time in order to fully experience that wellness.

Huh?

You asked, and Source gave, but you weren't standing on the bull's eye – so you jerked yourself over to where you wanted to be, and you did it so fast, it made your head spin.

So when I thought I had mono that one time…

One time? Try every few years. You had mono as a teen, but have you had it since?

No.

So then, you "thought" you had mono, even though you knew you didn't.

Well, I was tired, and it certainly felt like mono.

So sleep. You don't need the excuse of illness to take care of yourself.

Yes, but…

Ah, the "but." See, you didn't "feel" into your feelings. You felt into your thoughts about your body – but not your true feelings. Your feelings are very powerful tools, but you felt into your thoughts instead of feeling into your feelings.

I get it, but only because I just experienced this. Let me see if I can say it in a clear way for the reader: "When I knew from my heart instead of my head, everything was absolutely wonderful." What I'd been doing for so long, was feeling into my head and asking, "How does that thought feel?"

Instead of just going with a feeling, I would bypass the heart and go straight to my head so I could analyze the thought and really mull it over.

And how did that mulling work out for you?

It really stressed me out.

Well, yeah. So what did you do?

I just had this moment where I let go of all of my thoughts, and when I did, I felt this great wave of peace sweep over me. It was awesome. In fact, I think I kind of got startled by how quickly my body went calm. The calmness scared me.

Because?

Because I had a thought about it?

Yep. That would be correct. Now, having thoughts certainly is not a bad thing. Thoughts create! But, can you see how thinking about your feelings would stall the creation of what you think you're asking for?

Well, back to the example you wanted to use. I came home from Christmas break, booked these two great jobs...

And then you thought "Shit. There's not going to be anymore."

Hey. Do you want me to tell the story?

Yes, sorry.

Well... I guess I thought, "Shit. There's not going to be anymore."

And what did that create?

Well, it was the darndest thing. Wouldn't you know, the foreign account that was supposed to pay such a huge amount, decided to space it out over time.

Okay, but get this right now; it didn't stop, did it?

No. It didn't.

So even though you let a little bit of hesitation and doubt come in, Source still delivered, right?

Yes. It took a little longer than it was supposed to, and I had to really go out on a limb by hiring an editor without having the cash in hand to pay him...

No. You had to decide. You had to decide to trust. You had to let go.

Wow. Even coming off of that example you clinched up pretty fast. Did you feel that?

Yeah. As soon as I wrote "Let go," it was like this instant "Don't let go!" from within.

What do you think that was?

Lack of trust?

Bingo. You're getting pretty good at this.

Chapter 5

Who do you say I am?

So, let's talk about trust for a little bit. If there is no separation, who or what are you not really in trust of? Biblically, go back to Exodus and Source asking Moses, "Who do you say I am?" This is a very important question because it tells you how you are defining your universe, and in turn it will show you how you are directing your energy. How are you defining the God that you are? What are you not in trust of? It can't be Source, because you are Source. It can't be of the Universe; you are the Universe. It can't be the Law of Attraction, because… ah. There it is.

Holy shit. I don't trust the Law of Attraction? You don't even have to say it: I am Self-Love!

But you see now we're getting someplace. If you don't trust that what you focus on will be created, can you see how that would cause you to move from your heart into your mind? Can you see how that judgment and separation could then enter the picture?

Yes, and what I just got is that the heart and the mind are really not separate either, are they?

No they are not.

There! Just now, what was the thought that you had.

I heard it was okay to take my break, so I started thinking about tonight.

And?

Well, Like I mentioned above, I've been "purging" for a few days, and I was supposed to have a date tonight. I feel bad about canceling, but at the same time, I don't really want to go out. I want to throw on a hoodie, put in a movie, and chill out by myself.

There are a few things going on, are you willing to explore them?

Sure.

Okay.

1.   You don't want to go.

2.   You are judging yourself for not wanting to go.

3.   You're afraid of what might happen if the other person were to know you don't want to go (because what if it makes him not want to go?!)

4. You are trying to stay in this purging so that you can have an excuse for getting what you want – which is to not go.

Uuuuuhhhhh. That's so messed up.

It's perfect. You're perfect. Can you see though how you're not trusting yourself?

Maybe… not really.

You consciously don't want to go out. You feel bad for going out because you still have feelings for your ex – which is really just number 4 dressed up in a different party suit. If you don't want to go out, why go out?

Well, I feel like if I don't go out, I'll be lonely.

You "feel" like that, or you "think" that? You think that, because you have a thought telling you if you stay in you'll never meet anyone and you'll die alone and miserable and broke. Well, that might be a bit of hyperbole, but you get the gist, right?

Yeah.

So feel into who you really are. Feel into pure Source. Is pure Source lonely? Does pure Source worry? Who does Source say it is? Get. Out. Of. Your. Head.

Hmm. Well, when I tune in to pure Source, it's like all of that stuff goes away.

Would you like to know what all four of those things above really mean?

...Maybe. (Pause)

I am self love. Okay. Yes.

It means you like the drama. Oh, we can feel you wanting to get up right now. Your energy feels like it's running right now, doesn't it?

Yes. It's like someone just pulled the fire alarm inside. What is that?

It is the lack of trust in pure love. Rather, it's the choice to trust the drama. You might even say it's your addiction to drama.

Well that's not cool. I don't want that.

You say that, but if we asked you to give it up right now, you'd break off a little piece and stick it in your pocket and take it with you.

Why would I do that? I don't want the drama!

Even in protesting the drama, you're still in the drama of drama. Don't get discouraged. We'll show you a way out. You're not the only one looking, either. Most of consciousness is ready to drop their baggage, they just don't quite trust yet.

If we told you that you could remedy every situation you deemed unpleasant in your life by being totally honest about everything with everyone, would you do it?

Yes.

So could you call your date and just be honest with him and say that you don't want to go out and that when or if you do decide to go out, you might feel uneasy because you also still have feelings for someone else? Even more to the point, could you tell him the other person is a woman?

Um, sure; I could do that. Or I could keep my dignity and my options. Honesty in this case would be relationship suicide… That's a bad example.

It's a perfect example. Why do you need an excuse?

I'm not making excuses. I don't feel well, so I don't want to go out.

Energetically, you don't want to go out, so you don't feel well. This has been a huge pattern in your life. We know you recognize it, but it might help others to explore your own "story" around illness and relationships.

You were premature by a whole month. Do you think that was some kind of coincidence? You know better.

We touched on this example in book one: "If you suffer, you get what you want, and what you want is love – but to get love, you have to suffer and sacrifice what you really want." That was a fairly large energy for you to move through as well as many readers. Here is yet another (which in some cases may be a direct creation of the preceding belief): "I don't want what I want." In other words, "God is always opposing me. I am Source in opposition to itself."

What would that look like played out in the physical world?

Using the previously held belief that you must suffer, let's use an example from your past:

In college, you drank and had a good time. You pretty much did and said whatever you felt like doing or saying without really caring what anyone thought. Then, you got dumped and noticed something strange.

Yeah. It was like that Family Guy episode where Peter is in jail with a guy who keeps trying to stab him. Eventually, that guy gets stabbed and says something to the effect of "Ouch. That really hurt. That's what I've been doing to people? Oh my God. That's aweful!"

And in fact, you created getting dumped before you even met the girl who dumped you.

Why would I do that?

The year before you met her, you switched schools. There was an incident after a party, and you decided that you'd had enough of "the bull shit" and wanted to go to a "real" school with less restriction. So, the next semester, you did. You left the state and were away from your physical home for really the first time in your life. You begin attending the University you always wanted to attend. You had plenty of friends. In essence, you suffered, got what you wanted, found love, but according to your belief, needed to suffer. So what happened?

I missed home. I started feeling bad all the time.

No. You had everything you wanted, and you missed the drama. Everything was going well. You loved your classes. Your grades were excellent. The social life was great, but where's the drama? You had love, but couldn't accept it without suffering.

This goes back to one of your final questions from book one, doesn't it?

Yes. "Could it all be all right?"

Well, I'd sure like it to be. I am Self-Love.

So, explain to me how all of this comes together using this example because I'm fascinated.

You missed the drama, so you created some by leaving and going back home.

But you went back to a place where people loved you and knew your worth. Where's the drama in that? Better create something to muck it up. Here: create a dramatic relationship. Repeat the pattern in every possible way. Give up what you really want so that you can suffer and get love, then lose the love so that you can suffer – because suffering brings you love. Think about it. You had given up the school you thought you wanted. You were starting to give up you – as in you began thinking of a career and settling down and not ever following your real dreams, wants, and desires, so you got a relationship that you felt you could martyr all of those things for, and then you had to give that up because your definition of love included suffering. By suffering the break up, you got extra close with some of your other friends, yet you did this by bonding over wounds.

Well, going back to trust, it kind of sounds like maybe I wouldn't want to trust the Universe that brought me all of that.

Why not? The universe was just delivering what you were energetically asking for. You brought you all of that <u>through</u> your beliefs. That relationship was one of the catalysts that eventually got you out to Los Angeles. Your whole life has been a series of catalysts. You have always wanted to write. You have always wanted to entertain. You have always wanted to be a star – Oh, had trouble writing that last one, didn't you?

I am Self-Love.

Indeed.

You recognize the suffering in your past, but have you ever stopped to consider just how well everything in your life has gone together? You wanted to go to SMU, and so you went. You never wanted to graduate from there and settle down. Feel into that, and you'll know it's true. That wasn't the life you wanted back then. You don't want it now, either. You wanted to go to Los Angeles, so you used the beliefs you held to put in motion the events that would create that. You needed to suffer to get what you wanted, so you got to experience a bad relationship and some health problems. Looking back, it took almost dying to get you to move, but didn't the old you die anyway? All of those limitations? Gone. All of those old prejudices and fears? Gone. You experienced a rebirth. You needed to suffer some more, so you went back and finished school (laughter). None of it was really so bad, was it? Sure, at the time it seemed horrible and life threatening in so many ways, but now? Can't you see how guided and taken care of you've always been?

Yeah. I really can. All of those things that I'd been pissed off about all those years, actually helped get me where I am today – which is a pretty awesome place, but where does not wanting what I want come in?

You wanted love, yet love caused suffering. "I want love, yet love causes suffering." You held that in order to get love, you had to suffer, which took you out of love. So according to your beliefs, wanting something often delivered the opposite effect, so the best way to get what you wanted, was to not allow yourself to want it. Relating this to the topic of the chapter it would look like, "I want to trust the Universe, but the Universe is not trustworthy. Therefore, I don't want what I want."

Now, you can manifest in any way you see fit to create. Look at the energy on Earth right now. People feel what people have always felt: the end is coming. Well, the end is never the end, is it? You always want more and more, and as an eternal being, you will always experience more and more, so guess what? You're going to experience this based on what you believe. You believed according to a certain set of beliefs, and your heart desired certain experiences. So, the two got together and created in a way you could receive.

Even within the context of who you loved in college these beliefs were in play. You met a girl and fell in love, but part of you was in love with the fact that you were able to love a woman so fully. Loving her meant an "escape" from what you saw as torment (the torment of your own freedom and sexuality – the freedom of limitless expression). She represented what looked good to you on paper – and we don't say that with any insult intended towards her. She gave you quite the gift of self discovery.

Well, truth be told, I've never really loved anyone to the extent that I loved her. But I can also see where I've not ever opened up to anyone either. After her, I met my first boyfriend. That didn't end well. Then, I dated a friend, and I had feelings for her, but mostly, I think I saw her as an excuse to not put myself out there.

Looking back, I can totally see the pattern of "wanting what I don't want" in my life, and I really do want it to stop.

So, no more excuses?

No more excuses. I want to allow myself to know my pure connection to Source at all times and to know that I can have and enjoy what I'm asking for without the drama. I am Source saying to myself, I am Self-Love.

And you have it all in this very moment. Look at Los Angeles as a metaphor. You didn't just move to a new state, you moved to a new place within your own being. You entered a new "state" of consciousness.

Cute.

California represented a place where you could be who you truly are and celebrate yourself in every way. And you wanted to physically experience that. So you see Source always knows what you want. It's not like you're in some evil game show where the host is trying to get you to mess up. Source wants to give you everything and as you can see in your own personal case, Source had to really fight you to get those things to you. You really fought for relationships you knew weren't what you really wanted – and again, we're not judging those relationships, but it's like physically needing water but drinking a soft drink instead because it tastes better. Sure, it may quench your thirst, but what you really need on a deeper level, is water.

The other day, a woman complained to me about how bloated she was. She said the pressure got worse whenever she drank carbonated beverages. I

asked her why she drank them if they made her feel
worse, and she said, "well, because I like them."

Right. Inherently most people are in tune with what they really truly desire, but they often reach for something else instead – be it a carbonated beverage, the wrong relationship, an unfulfilling job, etc.

Knowing what you know now and having the gift of "hind-sight," can you maybe just trust from now on?

Yes.

Good. So, you see how trust plays into creation? Not trusting is a waste of time. The Law of Attraction always brings you what you want – always. Sometimes you judge the packaging as good or bad or unpleasant, etc, but it always delivers. If you can trust with absolute certainty that Source will always get you where you want to go, doesn't that feel like knowing?

Well, it feels like knowing.

So why would it be anything else? Back to college, your feelings said, "I want to go to Southern Methodist University. I want to live in Dallas." Your thoughts then jumped in and judged what that looked like. Your feelings said, "I want to go to California and write and live my life to the fullest," and your thoughts came in and took you in a direction where that wasn't enough.

Okay. I'm sorry if I'm the only one who is missing something here, but isn't it my thoughts that create my reality?

(Pause)

Ohhhhhhhh. So, what I'm thinking of as thoughts aren't actually thoughts at all. They're judgments.

Ding-ding-ding. You win the pony.

Holy shit. That's huge.

So you can see why we've been telling you to get out of your head.

So, clear this up for me: how did we even get here?

Look at this example from book one:

We told you, "Your thoughts form the waves that guide your consciousness into the potentiality of your directing. The waves then form the frequencies, which form the vibrations, which form the frequencies, etc. which creates or brings in the outer experience."

Before we move through this explanation, please claim "I am self Love" as we are about to move much of consciousness.

I am Self-Love.

Thank you.

Your thoughts come from your Source. Your feelings come from the waves that are formed from those thoughts. If judgment is present, as it has been, there is discord in the vibrations. This discord has confusingly been mistaken for thought.

I understand. "Judge not, lest ye be judged!"

Yes. The commandment has been interpreted as "If you judge, I (the great Creator God") will judge you. The missing piece has been that you are that great creator God, and you are all things, so in judging one, you judge the all – which you are. You are only ever judging yourself. You are saying, "I am God judging my creation" – which is to say, "I am judging what I am."

Here is a perfectly synchronistic example. What did you just do?

I just responded to an annoying text from a friend.

What was his text?

He asked me what I thought about aliens.

What was your response?

I just wrote back, "I don't."

And?

And in my head I was kind of like, "what a weird-o."

So, you judged him?

...Yes. I didn't mean to. I just kind of went, "what are you asking?" It turned out he was watching something about aliens and 2012. He knows that I think everything is energy, and that everything is all part of The One – so if there are aliens, cool. Same rules apply. If not, that's cool too.

Yet, you judged him for what you perceived to be his lack of knowing when it comes to that concept. If you look at your answer you will see why you judged him.

Because I "think" everything is energy?

Yes. Your judgment of him came from the place in you that says, "I *think* this, but I don't know this." This reflects an inner belief which is really a judgment that to know is better than not to know. There is a difference between saying, "I have a desire to experience knowing," and "I want to know because knowing is better than not knowing. In fact, knowing is good and not knowing is bad."

Let us take you down this road in another manner. You not multi-dimensionally, correct?

Correct.

To someone who doesn't see this way, could what you see be termed alien?

I guess, but that's what I tried to explain to him. Everything is all one consciousness.

Imagine for a second that you asked an infant to read you today's news. Would you get mad or judge that infant for not being able to read?

No. That's a seemingly unreal expectation.

It's not because it is an unreal expectation that you don't judge. You simply know the baby is where the baby is, developmentally speaking, and that's okay with you. Were that baby able to fulfill that request, you would judge that as astounding because it would in fact exceed your expectation. Again, your expectations are always in relation to your own experience.

But I thought this wasn't about expectation.

It's not about expectation with regard to "them" – meaning the baby or your friend. You always judge in relation to self. What we mean here is you would not judge the baby because you've asked a task you would not expect it to fulfill based on your own experience. You judged your friend for his lack of belief, not because he didn't believe, but because you wouldn't allow him to be where he was with regard to his understanding of consciousness and energy. You deemed his understanding wrong. On some level, his "not knowing" plugged you in.

Yes, but I know that everything is energy...

Yes, and you judged him for not knowing – which caused you to judge yourself because you still hold that judgment is bad. What we are trying to show you is that in judgment itself is the implicitness of good/bad, right/wrong. You judged him for not knowing, and then you judged yourself, and then you turned your judgment back to him for "making you" judge yourself. We use that term "making you" because this is how most people feel in these situations. They feel that under normal circumstances, they would have behaved in one manner, but some person has "made them" feel another way by their actions. They've been "forced into" a feeling. Hence, "judge not, lest ye be judged." All judgment comes back to you because you are all things. If you judge anything as wrong, you are also saying that means there is right. Therefore, if there is right and wrong, your own action must fall into these categories as well. Judgment is the surest way to set yourself up for failure.

Well, how does this relate to the whole?

100

Look at your world. Economically, do you feel it's better to be rich or poor? Religiously, is it better to be Christian than to be Muslim? Is Atheism a better choice than Buddhism? Is America a more righteous nation than any other? These are all questions that could not arise in an environment where judgment was not present. Interestingly enough, there is not only judgment present in these questions, but also comparison.

And that's bad?

It's neither bad nor good. However, comparison in these cases comes with its own sense of powerlessness.

I don't think I understand that.

If you knew that what you know was what created your reality – and that you were the only person who was able to do this – would you ever feel threatened by another's ideology?

No; I guess not.

So you see, when you set things up against each other, you do so in order to prove one way superior or correct. To a Muslim, the Muslim way is correct. To a Christian, the Christian way is correct, and so forth.

Yes, but what if implicit in one religion is that all other religions are wrong?

No one can create for you other than you. If you find yourself in a situation where conflict is present, that conflict represents a deeper issue within your own consciousness. Remember, there is no right or wrong in the larger sense. Everything experienced in the physical comes from vibration in the non-physical. This is why Self-Love is so important to someone wishing to experience unity and peace.

Yes, but once again... how can I say this and stay on topic? If someone else only accomplishes their goals by denying me my own, how can I simply go on about my business?

Let's explore that with regard to the idea of control, shall we?

Chapter Six

God as Control

In order to fully examine the idea of God held by consciousness, we must look to the birth of "God" as a creator with Sovereign power over all.

Okay. Well, where would you like to start?

You asked us how you could create something that was in direct opposition to someone else's desires. The simple answer is: focus on what you want, and create it. However, knowing that all outer strife is the manifestation of an inner conflict, we will discuss this issue with you in greater detail.

A consciousness that does not trust itself as God will create an exterior force to command it.

This is why we addressed the fear of creation in the first book, right?

Yes. Now, taking the above statement as fact, you can then trace the development of good/evil, God/Devil. They both serve the same function. The good/God force serves to command and enforce a certain moral code. The evil/Devil energy motivates one to follow that order as well as offering a viable excuse as to why that good/God force might be questioned. In other words, "I am not questioning

God. The Devil is making me" or "God did not do this; it was the Devil." This type of structure leads one to cling even stronger to the notion of God. "If I let go, the devil will get me." The fear perpetuates that need for an outside creative force.

So we control our own consciousness by taking away our control?

Yes, and you have actually taken nothing away from yourself. You have simply set up a new structure in which you can explore yourself while avoiding creative responsibility.

Why would consciousness choose to do that? Why couldn't we just know all there is to know? Is it because of fear?

That's one answer. Yet choosing to explore oneself as an individualized system operating according to the will of another can also be looked at simply as a way for Source to further explore itself. Look at it in simple factual terms: You were Source energy that came forth to experience physical being. You chose to become an individualized expression so that you could fully explore your own facet – which might include exploring fear. Remember, Source is not bothered by fear because Source knows itself at all times. The individualized expression is the only part which experiences separation and fear – both of which are illusion (just as the individual self is an illusion). Yet, this illusion became God, and as such, needed to be maintained at all times.

What do you mean by "this illusion became God?"

The illusion of separation literally became God. Mankind began serving an illusion and gave its power away because it feared its own creative authority and responsibility.

Why?

Let's go back to the example of worshipping the God of victimization. If an event happens that your individualized self doesn't like, will it be easier for that self to accept that the event happened as the result of the will of a greater force who wields power over all, whose motives must never be questioned, and who somehow has a plan for this event to work for good? Or that the event occurred because of an active vibration within the self's system? In other words, why take responsibility when you can chalk it up to divine will?

Option one strokes the ego and allows for self-importance, while option two seems cold and sterile. People often don't expect random acts of good fortune to befall them. They don't sit around thinking about all the possible bounty that might come to them at any moment. Yet, they constantly allow their thoughts to dwell on things they don't want. Is it any wonder that these things then occur? Your physical environment is proof of what you think about, not the other way around. When something bad happens, how often do you find yourself saying, "I knew that would happen?" In the context of this kind of thinking, it becomes extremely important that the self be kept small because the self knows bad things will occur. It needs to be kept in check to ensure safety and survival.

Why on earth would anyone choose to worship that kind of illusion?

Because the fear within that illusion is like a strong magnet, and once you find yourself pulled in and focused on the fear, more and more shows up to validate the illusion of separation. Eventually, you don't even know you're serving an illusion because the fear has become so real. Consciousness literally becomes scared to death to remember its divine nature.

What do you mean literally?

It's blasphemy in almost all religions to know yourself as God. To most, blasphemy equals eternal damnation. What better deterrent?

106

Again, this isn't a bad thing. It's simply how consciousness has chosen to experience itself. Now, however, consciousness wants to experience something else.

Then why couldn't there just be an instant evolution? Why does consciousness need the individual selves to choose?

Do you need the consciousness to evolve before you choose, or can you evolve independently?

Independently.

So then do you understand the answer to your question?

Umm... no.

Must you create in order to know you are creator?

Well, yes. If I'm not creating, wouldn't that show me in fact that I am not the creator of my reality?

The physical is simply a mirror of the beliefs and thought patterns you hold. If you believe you are not the creator, your world will show up in a way that validates this belief.

Like the four minute mile?

107

Yes. If you know that you create your world – really know it at the vibratory level of being – your world will mirror this knowing back to you.

So again, we're back to "as I believe?"

Do you believe that consciousness can change with one person, or do you believe that consciousness is bigger than one individual self?

...Both.

So then you see the confusion that exists. If the answer is both, then the evolution will take place, but it will take place as an event of momentum because it must take place while honoring the individualized aspects. Those aspects will also be influenced by the mass, and therefore, the individual choices become important and valid because the mass shift can only happen when the single shift occurs.

I think you just gave us the metaphysical equivalent of "which came first: the chicken or the egg?"

But can you see how both sides are honored? In the grand scheme, Source is Source. Where you are right now, appears to be a linear point in conscious time, but in actuality, it is a part of a bigger and simultaneous whole. Consciousness is exploring itself as both the result of the collective individual aspects as well as the individual resulting from the collective.

In English?

Consciousness is experiencing itself as the whole that is influenced by the individual as well as the individual which is influenced by the whole.

So which one really counts?

Both. Look at it in terms of control. People tend to want others to be in control.

I'm not sure I buy that argument.

What is religion? What are politics?

Systems of... Okay. You got me. They both enable people to pass the buck.

Again, that's not a bad thing. Thousands of years ago, consciousness was not evolved to the point of being self aware. Mankind didn't know itself as spiritual. Systems enabled expansion in some areas and ensured physical survival in others. Even today, people want their rulers to take care of their overall world-events so that they can focus their own creative time on what they see as their immediate world.

I can feel myself wanting to point out how governments and religions use limiting ideas or fear to control people, so I'm going to take this opportunity to claim Self-Love before we move on.

Indeed. Remember no one can be controlled. Every situation emerges as the result of an authored energy. What we mean by that is every situation is the physical match to non-physical vibration.

In other words, if I'm in a situation – whether I perceive it as good or bad – I'm there because it's a physical match to my own energy?

Yes. Now, as a whole, consciousness is reaching a point where it no longer wishes to be limited. Religion and government have served their purposes.

Speaking of, I really thought this was going to be a discussion about religion.

It's a discussion about the religion of consciousness. That's not a "religion" as you know it, but rather a stance with regard to what authors creation. Consciousness – both collective and individual – is asking to remember who it is. You've asked, "Why can't it just happen" which is the same as asking, "Why can't God just choose to make it happen?" The answer is God does choose. God chooses through you and as you, because there is no separation.

110

The memory of creation is being stirred in a major way, yet the walls that have been put up must first come down. Included in these walls are fears and judgments that keep everyone separate. So you see, consciousness right now on this planet is like a ball of string. It's all one, but it's a little tied up and knotted. What we're here to do is discuss why it became knotted, how to unknot it, and how to physically move into a new era.

Okay. So, let's recap. How did we get to this place?

The old divide and conquer attitude. Consciousness as a whole said, "I will be easier to control if I split off from my Self. I can divide myself into tiny parts, and I can then rule over these parts.

That sounds kind of Tudor-ish of us.

Indeed. You're making historical reference to King Henry VIII, but it's a relevant observation as all events are the physical manifestation of consciousness.

That's a nice way to explain history.

There's no judgment. Events happen as a reflection of the consciousness involved. Often times, these events are the direct result of the attachment to control. Take for example the Salem witch trials. Many of the people who were burned or hung were not witches, nor did they possess any modicum of what today would be termed "psychic" ability. They were simply in the way of someone else's desire for power or morality or… fill in the blank.

That goes back to my question from the end of the last chapter.

It also goes back to our answer about consciousness as a whole and as a collaborative effect of individuality. There has to be total balance and love in the non-physical plane for there to be total balance and love on the physical plane. This is one of the reasons religion is so hard to give up. You'll notice we said religion and not God. No one must ever give up God, for how could anyone give up that which they are? However, many people confuse God with religion.

Why is that?

The most common reason is that divinity is often expressed through the stories of religious texts. There is no discernable way to remove God from the story, because God is the story. We say God here meaning a perceived God, not Source.

Why would we create God in our image?

112

In some cases this creation helps people understand who they are, and in others, it prevents them from having to know who they are.

I suppose it could also help justify seemingly unjustifiable action.

It has served that end as well. Remember though, don't judge anyone for their beliefs about God, for any belief serves the One in that it provides a system of Self exploration. This is hard to allow when you don't understand that you are the only creative force at work in your world.

When everyone knows that, there will be peace on earth. No one will need to take from another. No one will need to control another or themselves.

What do you mean themselves?

If you are the only creative force in your world, yet someone else is given power over you, you are in effect controlling yourself by allowing another to create for you.

That seems really backwards.

Yes, it does. But again, perceptually, the belief holds that you can either be conquered by God, by your self, or by someone else. At the level of Source, it's all the same. There is no separation. Consciousness would like to remove the barriers it has put up. It would like to release control, and it will start to do this by calling out at as a collective and gathering individual responses. Again, this will cause the momentum that will allow a greater shift in the whole, which will allow more individuals to break their old energy cycles, etc.

What just struck me was that this is kind of the story of individual ascension just on a larger scale.

Yes. You break down beliefs and expand and evolve until you remember your oneness with Source. The consciousness does the same. The individuals are like cells in a body. Everyone communicates and operates as a part of a larger whole.

So relate all of this to God as Control.

Well, we've been discussing religion and definitions of God, and what better example? Within the context of religion, one has the ability to control God, control others, and control the self. God is controlled because conceptually, "God" is now a known entity within a finite structure. Rules are established which then enable codes to be enforced. People are divided into groups, those groups into subgroups – all according to God's will. In truth, it actually is according to God's will, just not an outside God separate from the self.

Meaning they create their own realities?

Indeed. People tend to get so angry about religion, but in truth as we said earlier, all religions come from a desire to know God -= which is really a desire to know the Self.

Well, I think the anger comes into play – like I said earlier – when people try and usurp the free will of others.

And again, no one can ever usurp the free will of any individual. There is only one presence acting anywhere, and that is God.

I think that kind of gets confusing because on the one hand, we're talking about how everyone is God, and on the other hand, there is only one God.

Think of God not as a person, but as an energy – an all pervading presence. Nothing exists other than God. Where you have seen personalities interacting with each other, see only God – made up in different form and interacting with Himself.

Like in "Men in Black" with the Edgar suit? The main character looked like Edgar, but it was really some other force inside, wearing him like a suit.

God is not a separate being "wearing" you. You are God experiencing an individualized existence wherein you are interacting with numerous other individualizations of the same Source. We feel the anger might subside were people to take their attention from limitation and lack and place it upon abundance, prosperity, and maybe even a little fun.

There is plenty God to go around. Much of the controlling aspects of God and religion have come from the feelings of abandonment, judgment, and lack which have in turn lead to feelings of abuse and neglect. Again, it is a brilliant system to look out upon and experience, yet consciousness is calling for something else.

A new start, the blank page?

And beyond. New thought. New creation. This is why we went to such lengths in book one to explain the significance of stories and creation. For most of consciousness, there is no bigger story to give up than the story of God and creation.

I have a feeling I already know the answer to this one, but how do we give that story up? How do we move into knowing who and what we are? How do we give up centuries of baggage around God and religion and even creation itself?

First of all, you will only be giving up centuries of baggage if you decide to put your belief in centuries of baggage. The only moment anyone will ever create in is the moment of now; now is the only moment present. Giving up a story is as easy as putting down a heavy weight you no longer wish to carry. In this case, that weight is familiar and we would go so far as to say that many people are in love with the weight – even though it causes them strain and drama. Aside from the willingness to release the weight – the story – one needs do nothing but love.

I am Self-Love?

Indeed. You see, there is but one kingdom just as there is but one energy and one Source. It is not separate from who you are. It is not a place only experienced after death. It requires no belief.

Then why do so many people believe there is only one way to God?

Because that is their truth. Some people are taught and socialized into their way, others experience sartorial events or "supernatural" happenings, but in reality, each person is the architect of their own beliefs. The monk reaching enlightenment on a hill is no different than a fundamentalist born into a religion they will never question. Socialization, learning, expansion: all are choices and all are valid experiences of individualization.

(Pause) Hit a nerve, did we?

I guess I'm just trying to comprehend how it is just as valid a choice or experience to really seek a higher understanding of God and the universe as it is to be born into something and just take it all in blindly.

In other words, you're having trouble letting go of judgment and separation? You realize those are two of the aspects of self that lead to that little control thing we were talking about earlier, don't you? From our vantage point, it's all good because again, it's all God.

It might help to release your attachment to control. You might actually begin with the reasons you've attached such importance to control in the first place, which leads us back to knowing the abundance of God – indeed knowing just how vast and great your own being is. Could you allow another their own individualized experience – or even a group of individuals their own group experience – if you knew that at all times you were in charge and safe?

Well of course I could, but the problem is, I live in the real world.

Ah, "the real world." And what happens in this "real world?"

Well, I don't want to hammer this one subject, but, like the bumper sticker says, "shit happens."

"Shit" never happens. You are always responsible for your creation. The belief that you are not is one of the main reasons religion and the concept of a creator God was born on this plane. Even if you consciously do not know you create, you do. Everything in your world is a match to your energy. You direct it always, and when you can know this and trust this – and by the way this is much easier to verify than you think. Just look back over your life. Consciousness has a concept of life after death that in the beginning was simply a healthy understanding of the eternal aspect of being, but later evolved to suit a consciousness that didn't quite trust it would always do the right thing. At the heart of every religion is the truth that all are one.

I don't know what Unitarian church you grew up in, but I was raised to believe that the only way you could get to heaven was through a personal relationship with Jesus Christ.

Luckily, you noticed there were some dead folks hanging around… We're kidding, but this is a perfect example of how no choice is better than any other. You are no better now than you were when you were entertaining thoughts of the priesthood. You are no more loved, nor are you any less loved.

119

You simply chose a path and explored that path. This is the freedom that should be granted to all beings. Jesus never said to believe in Him. Yes, he said "I am" the way the truth and the life, and that no man would come to the father but through Him, but he was really addressing the same principle we are. No one may know their oneness with Source unless they know their own "I AM" presence – the presence of God in all that is all. When specifically asked about heaven, he never said it was a place.

He did say there were many mansions…

And indeed you are one of those mansions. Within the one house of consciousness are many houses of consciousness. He used the metaphor of mansions and houses as we have used cells in a body. The truth is the same.

That does make sense when I think about what He actually said in the Bible about getting access to the kingdom. He said that all anyone must do is love God with all their heart and love their neighbor as themselves.

Because they are all one. Knowing that, can you begin to release having to control others and their choices? We are not saying allow someone to walk all over you – unless that is what you wish to experience. We are simply saying that there is room for everyone's belief. If you want to see change in

120

your environment, be that change. See it everywhere, and love everyone and everything. Celebrate God because God is everywhere and God is everything. When you can know that, you will no longer see lack or limitation. You will no longer feel the need to judge or change anyone or anything. You will see the perfection of everything.

That's a pretty tall order, but one I'm ready to fill.

Luckily, the kitchen is always open.

Chapter 7

Starting from the End

That's an interesting chapter title. I thought everything was now.

Indeed.

Okay... but if now is all there is, how can there ever be an ending?

That's a very good question, and one that actually reveals more about perception than most might consciously be aware.

What do you mean by that?

Well, there will <u>never</u> be an end – that's true: Expansion is eternal. However, expansion doesn't mean learning lessons or experiencing a down so that you can enjoy the up. It <u>can</u> mean those things, but it doesn't have to. It can also mean the constant fulfillment of desire, or the eternal experience and expression of love.

I'm going to stop you right there because as soon as I read those words my first thought was, "How boring?"

This will reveal a lot.

How do you mean?

Well, if completion is looked upon with any kind of negative gaze, and you're bringing forth into manifestation only the things that vibrationally stoke your boat, you're probably not going to be completing things anytime soon, are you?

Well...

(Interrupting) Save up a little bit of money... Oh. Now you have to fix your car. Save up a little more money... Oh. Now there's a plumbing issue; there goes that rainy day fund. Save up a little bit of money.... Oh. Now your stocks have fallen, and your investments are worthless... "I guess I'll just have to keep on working and not ever retire."

I am Self-Love!

(Laughing) Indeed! And you know those limitations aren't just held with regard to money. Some people have plenty of money, but their relationships aren't ever at that 100 per cent mark. Some people have money and relationships, but just aren't happy with the way they look or the way the world looks: "It's always something!"

You've heard that phrase no doubt many times before; you may have even used it a few times. Well, the fear of completion is where this actually comes from. Because if you wanted to be complete –if you really wanted all the money you wanted, or really wanted all the relationships you wanted, wouldn't you have them – wouldn't you be complete?

Well, this is part of the problem I think a lot of people – including me – have with things like The Secret and the idea of the Law of Attraction. According to the Law of Attraction, all I have to do is want it badly enough.

Ah. What a major misconception. First of all, it's not from a place of wanting that you create – nor is it <u>not</u> from that place. The wanting is simply a manifestation of or a noticing of something you now desire, but do not yet have. Now, sometimes, the vibration of wanting is actually a vibration of lack. "I want this" means "I've noticed I don't have this, and I'm not complete without it." Therefore, "getting" becomes very important because you must be whole, right?

Wrong. It's a very impressive game, but if you fear completion or feel – as you said – like it might be boring to just sit around and have everything you want, why on earth would you then come forward and complete yourself in any of these areas (money, relationships, etc)? The answer is, you wouldn't, and you won't!

Well that sucks.

Only because you don't realize you're already whole in every moment.

Okay, but again, that sounds like a cop-out. It's like, "well, I really want this, but I'm already whole, so I guess I don't need it – oh look, it's not showing up just like I directed!" It just seems like a lot of double talk.

We know. We see exactly where you are right now, and we understand. Just take a deep breath and prepare to move beyond all the limiting stories you've got about the Law of Attraction.

You see, the Law of Attraction is not God. It's not outside of you. It just is, and it is a part of the very fabric of who you are. So don't get mad at it. "It" didn't do anything. It's just words used to express your own avenues of creation.

Now, you are whole in every moment.

We've been over this…

I am Self-Love.

Thank you.

What happens in scenarios like these are that you begin to feel like you're not whole. "I must have a relationship and then everything will be as I'd like it to be." Or, "I must have this amount of money." This is a much different vibration than knowing you're already whole and you love and accept yourself and because of this love, you're allowing yourself to explore new and fun avenues of Self Creation such as relationships and money.

We said this in book one, but when you're in love with someone, you usually have the urge to give to them – whether it be emotional support or physical gifts. It's the same when you love yourself. You want to give yourself everything you want. And because you're complete, there's no gap between what you want and what you have.

What do you mean?

You're constantly whole and expanding. You're in a state of pure grace – and we say "grace" here meaning that you've moved out of your own way, released your own stories, and given over fully to the largest and grandest love of which you are. In this state, you ask and receive. The two become one. As the differing aspects of you expand, so does your world. No part of you is left unfulfilled.

Differing aspects?

Sure. You have multiple desires. The whole point of book one was to move into a state of total Self love so you could just "go with the flow." When you're in the flow, you're one with all your desires because the desires aren't coming from a need to define who or what you are; they're coming from a natural, child-like want.

Come as a child...

Exactly. There's an innocent, exuberant, and loving quality of wonder around everything, and the universe rushes in to meet that wonder with experiences that serve to fulfill your desires and answer your questions. The Kingdom of heaven becomes apparent both within and without. God is seen everywhere – including the self.

So, relate that to the title of this chapter.

Well, in that child-like faith is a certain degree of knowing. Kids often "want something so bad they can feel it." Well, truly feeling it is starting at the end. When you start your desire from this place, the Universe has no other option but to swoop in and deliver more of that vibration.

So often in the old ways of thinking, people wanted something or someone because of a feeling they sought. There was a belief that said, "I will not be happy without this thing, this person, or this situation." What is coming about now, is the advent of a new thought with regard to desire. There does not have to be a realization of lack within want. You can simply decide you want something and bring it about by feeling it as it already is.

Feelings are great, but what about necessities. This is all great when we're talking about getting a job or finding a loving relationship, but what about people who need food or water.

Need is an aspect that contains a story. Yes, physicality requires sustenance, but to need it implies a lack or restriction on some level – just as wanting in fact still implies "it's not here" within the energetic hologram of most.

Okay. I think we just branched off into another subject, and I don't feel my initial question has been answered to my satisfaction.

Indeed. We just said you could "simply decide you want something and bring it about by feeling it as it already is," and then seemingly contradicted that statement by telling you that *wanting* still implies a focus on or knowing of incompleteness.

Think of it this way: If you were incredibly hungry and really wanted a sandwich, and you were then given a sandwich, would you continue wanting the sandwich?

This is actually very interesting. You're talking about sandwiches, but I wandered into the example of money, and my initial answer is twofold: I would take the money, and I would continue wanting more.

Then you see you've never fully received the gift you were given and will therefore repeat the pattern of want.

We used the example of a sandwich because you can physically eat it, break it down, and feel it fill you up and energize you. Money, food, it's all energy, but we used food because of its association with biology and the continuation of life.

In a balanced energy system, a want is formed and you ask…

Maybe we should scrub the term "want" and replace it with desire…

We could replace it with any word, but so long as the energy or motivational pattern of fulfillment went unchanged, the end result would be the same.

In a balanced system, you want, you ask, you receive.

"Ask and it is given."

I remember reading that the interpretation for the word "ask" in that verse is a Biblical misinterpretation. The Aramaic verse used the word " sha'al" which meant to ask, but also meant, demand, lay claim to, and require.

Yes. Asking is not a meek act. It is an act of courageous faith and knowing. Asking is a presigned vibrational contract with the Universe. This is why so much stress has been put on phrases like "Go with the flow," "Let go and let God," Less of me and more of Thee." They are all semantically saying "Get my shit out of the way so I can receive the abundance that the Universe has ready for me." Another aspect to this can be seen in the anecdote "God helps those who help themselves."

Those who help themselves are fulfilling part of the law. They are "laying claim" to that which they want. So with this understanding, "ask" becomes a vibrationally empowered word. The meaning changes; it is no longer a passive act; it is a powerful claim to one's own creational abilities and innate rights as manifested aspects of Source.

Now, the other "branch" you mentioned was what we called your hologram – which also goes along with what we termed your "motivational pattern of fulfillment."

We spoke in book one about pixels, pictures, and ultimately we touched on the notion that everything is a type of energetic hologram. Now, we know some have taken this literally to mean that the entire world is "fake," but what we'd like to make clear is that we're not so much talking about "real" vs "fake" as it's understood on your plane so much as

we're saying "it's all fake, and it's all real."
Perspective and choice rule the day.

Let's say The Alpha and The Omega are contained within One Hologram – by the way, you're capitalizing those words, not us. Notice we also said "One" hologram and not "The One" hologram. If you'll let this sink in, your mind might be rocked.

Whoa... I just remembered our discussion in Love, Life, God about infinite fields and possibilities.

Exactly; now within this one hologram is the beginning and the end – again, there is no beginning, and there is no end, but think of it in perceptual linear terms.

Like: Jarrad Hewett was born inside of Mercy Hospital on January 14th, 1979? That's perceptually the beginning of me, right?

Most people would consider that your beginning, yes. But what about this: Your linear story really begins thousands and thousands (and thousands) of years ago. How many people came together, and pro-created (whether wed or unwed, by choice or through seeming "force") in order to bring about the realized potential that birthed that day? You see, your hologram (your story of existence as Jarrad) seemingly begins on January 14th, 1979, or maybe even with conception, or with the meeting of your parents. In fact, your story is contained inside an even greater story which includes everything that came before, and everything that will come after. Every single thing you have ever done or not done for that matter has had an effect on the collective experience.

Talk about a butterfly effect... So how does this relate to asking or starting from the end?

If you can **imagine** a hologram large enough to contain every other hologram, and then literally allow for expansion within and without of that hologram – while knowing that even the largest possible hologram is contained in a sub-field of its own, you begin to see just how vast creation is. You begin to see how it becomes possible for each person to live every moment as a moment of choice. Every moment is a fractal of a larger moment, and within that larger moment, all moments exist. The moment exists that created desire, and the moment exists where that desire was fulfilled to its greatest degree. What is "real" is the choice you make and which moment you choose to experience.

This is some really amazing shit!

Isn't it?

When you ask for something, know everything we just said. Use that knowledge to help guide you into the actualized and fulfilled potential of whatever it is you wish to experience. Know also, that when you ask and receive, you've just started, ended, and begun a new story.

Aren't we always trying to lose our story so that we can expand?

Only lose the stories you don't enjoy. This is one topic that is often taken to extremes by teachers who understand the intention, but haven't quite come to understand that expansion happens not just in letting go of definition, but also in reveling in it.

Can you explain that a little bit?

(As a joke, "The end" by The Doors began to play)

That wasn't actually a joke. THIS is the END. This is where we want you to start from. You see, book one involved letting go of stories that were limiting. What we're bringing up now is the concept that desire is a story. That story can end with fulfillment. Asking from that place of knowing and fulfillment helps facilitate the change of story you are asking for. Now, if fulfillment brings you joy and love, by all means, ride that wave until a new desire springs up, then rinse, repeat.

Some people who are asking to expand are also stuck in an unbalanced field of motivational pattern fulfillment. In other words, they are experiencing a type of fulfillment by constantly bringing up stories to let go of. They are kicking themselves over what a hard process releasing is, and we are simply offering to them the idea that they can also release the need to release – because in doing so, everything they wish to release will also release.

We'd also like to offer that what they are experiencing is not bad (or good for that matter); it simply is. It is their experience. Often times this experience comes forward as one last hurdle to overcome – and interestingly enough (or not), it is often the product of a belief system that says, "Almost… one last hurdle."

We'll probe a little further using you as an example, if you don't mind.

Not at all.

Well, using your own story, your "one last hurdle" has involved religion – hence the experience of this book. You're not just writing to write. You're not even writing just to expand your own awareness. You are actually writing as a way of releasing the entire "muck" you've collected around religion and are thus entering into a new, more expansive and freer story. Your "last hurdle" has actually been a hologram containing smaller holograms filled with stories of right and wrong, judgment and non-judgment, duality and non-duality, balance, polarity and division, sexuality, attachment, break-ups, heart ache, and more. All of these actually come from religion – whether genetically (ie: the religion of family) or otherwise.

Can we stop there and take a look at what that last sentence means?

Absolutely; in fact, isn't there something you'd like to do?

In fact there is...

Chapter 8

Religion and Sexuality

Well done.

Thank you. I REALLY wanted to title a chapter.

You're getting the hang of this.

Now, you wanted to discuss "genetic" religion and also what we termed as "other" religion. What we'd like to start out with is an explanation that "religion" is anything you are devoted to. This understanding will make the term much easier to process and understand.

Okay, so when I hear the term "genetic," I tend to think of things that are literally a part of my physical make-up – something is literally in my genes.

That's partly true. The statement itself holds water – pardon the pun – but the truth is genes are alterable. If everything that exists is a physical representation of a hologram or an energy, at some level – whether conscious or not (as far as you would understand that term) – the energetic make-up can be changed, therefore the physical reality can be altered.

I thought that stuff was permanent.

What, your genes?

Yeah.

To quote a country song, "The only thing that stays the same is everything changes."

I don't want to get too off track, but is that really true?

Well, at one level it is, and at another level it isn't. Remember the line from *Almost Famous,* "It's all happening?" Well, it is. All of it – whatever that is, whatever that isn't. Love is certainly constant, though on more perceptually separated levels of being, love is also a choice. So even though there is a constant, there is an option to accept the constant, or reject it.

This is actually a great segue into genetic religion.

We're about to get trippy, aren't we? I just saw a giant ball of light... We're going all the way back for this one, aren't we?

The perceived beginning, yes. There was a time – for lack of a better term – I guess we could better phrase that, "There was a point in creation," where the greater you became self-aware. If you'll follow the punctuation, the Self became self-aware. Before

138

this point, there was only Self-awareness, but at some point – and the point is both different and the same for all beings – creation became aware of itself.

Can we use the word Source?

Yes, all though Source has always been aware of its Self. What we're talking about here is the moment when Source began experiencing itself in individualized "separate" ways from the whole of its Self. In a way, Source became an observer of self – small s. This self, then became self-aware. Now, this awareness didn't happen overnight (and it did). There were varying linear stages of human progression, certainly, but we're talking about self beyond the human scope.

Think of Source in terms of "creator." Source creates a cell – or a ball of light. That cell or ball of light then splits in two. Those two balls or cells then also split, and so on and so forth. Now, genetically, you know you have a set of great, great, great, great, great, great grandparents, but you don't know them. You know logically that they must have been there – they must have existed, but you don't really know who they were, what they did, etc. The smaller self works much the same way with relation to Source. You are living out so many existences and so many lifetimes in so many places and on so many levels,

139

that sometimes the smaller self loses track of its origin. It feels like it is so far removed from where it really came from, that it needs to find some way back. The easiest way back is to know you never left in the first place, but we understand that from the human perspective, things don't always feel, look, or seem as easy as they really are. In fact, this is a great place to mention the ego because it is the ego that both gives you the experience of definition, of a linear self, and that can also hinder your ability to transcend the gifted experience you came here to have.

I still don't understand why anyone would choose to come to earth – or incarnate anywhere if you want to be as broad and open about this as possible – and then experience a lifetime of separation with such a desire present to be one. Why do people choose to feel the pain of separation or loss? Why would anyone choose to feel alone?

The short answer would be that the answer is in the question: it is simply a choice.

Well, give me the long answer.

Have you ever thought about doing something – wondered what an experience would be like – but decided not to do it because you thought the experience might not be fun?

Absolutely.

What about the same question, just substitute the word "rewarding" for "fun?"

Definitely.

Well, as Source, you don't ever really take any of that into consideration. See, you're asking questions that need to be satisfied on a mind basis – in other words, you're asking this question from a limited perspective.

As Einstein put it, "You can't solve a problem with the same mind that created it," right?

Exactly. Now, we understand that the point of these conversations is to educate the soul and help ease the reader into a transcendent state, so we'll certainly continue, but more than anything, you have to understand that as Source, you've got all the options covered. You're looking out into life – we'll call life separation here, because to a lot of people on this plane, maybe even most, that's what life sometimes feels like – and you're seeing every possibility, every outcome, every moment of joy, happiness, grief, sorrow, love, loss, etc, and you're seeing it not in the context of human understanding but through the lens of ever-expanding Self knowledge and understanding. It's the equivalent of playing a game of tennis, or running a mile, or even

141

watching a great movie (or a bad one for that matter). You might miss a point. You might step over the line. You might get a penalty called. You might pull a muscle. You might cry. You might laugh. You might fall in love, or you might just change your mind half-way through and decide to go do something else. It really doesn't matter – and it does. All you're here for is the experience. The idea that the experience has a right or a wrong, that there is any particular thing to do, and that if you don't do that thing and you DO get it wrong that you'll suffer an endless death in fire or that you'll cease to be – those ideas do not help people on this plane. They don't! Not anymore.

I think I might be lost.

Just keep typing. You're not lost. You've just stepped out of your mind for a minute, so it's hard to keep up with what's coming out on the page.

Some people play games because they want to win. Why do they want to win? Ultimately, we hope it's because they like the feeling it gives them. Even if someone plays to win because they'll die if they don't, they're still playing because of a feeling; they like the feeling of being alive, so they play to win. Even if they play to win because they're afraid they'll lose approval or love or fill-in-the-blank if they lose, they play to win because they like the way

142

love and approval and fill-in-the-blank makes them feel.

People do things because they like the way those things make them feel.

How does that fit in with the title of the chapter and what we've been talking about?

It feels good to be connected to God. It feels good to know – from an ego perspective or a limited perspective of separation – that God is on your side. It feels good to know there is a God and that there is order to the Universe. Genetically, you're programmed to remember connection because from whence everything and everyone is, there is no separation. Connection can only exist within the perception of separation, because without that polarity, everything is just is, and it "just is" as one.

Right there – you had a light-bulb moment.

It just dawned on me that even the act of disconnecting serves more of a purpose than just the individual experience. It gives birth to the knowledge of Oneness.

The light and the dark are one.

My mind just hit a stopping point. Isaah 45:7 says (God speaking) "I form the light, and create darkness: I make peace, and create evil..." I used to think that the dark – so to speak – was the turning away from the light, but what I just realized is, you can't create darkness in a lit room.

No, but you could close your eyes. And that's what many people do. But we don't want to get too far ahead of ourselves. You see, people think that the light and the dark are one, but realize also that light and dark are two perspectives that help to draw awareness to each other. The concept of light and dark exist outside of the One true awareness – the original Source from whence we all are. There is only light there, and on some level, every living organism knows it. You can feel it. Just sit still for a moment and breathe.

I'm not a big fan of relaxation techniques. I mean, I am, but only when I want to relax. I don't find they do me too much good when I'm in an immediate state of ...something else.

It's not a technique. It's a knowing.

This actually brings us to the point of sexuality.

Nice.

Not like that.

Damn.

Oh, we can get into that, but we want to first talk about gender.

144

Oh, as in like, what sex are you?

Sort of.

Source is neither male nor female. People tend to see God as a patriarchal figure. This doesn't reflect Source so much as it reflects the consciousness' ideas about itself, about society, and about its own specific roles, freedoms, and limitations.

There is this idea prevalent in many religions that man has dominion over everything – including females. As we discussed in the first few pages, this is simply a reflection of the consciousness through which evolution occurred. If we were trying to speak to you five thousand years ago about complex computer models, you wouldn't have known what we were talking about. We could have given you words, but you might not have really truly understood what we were saying.

Jesus himself said much of the same thing. He told his disciples that even they wouldn't understand most of what he was teaching.

Indeed. One such parable is the story of heaven: "In my Father's house are many mansions." The Father's house is all of creation. Father was chosen because that was the understood image of God. In all of creation, the house, there are many mansions. You have the ability to be whatever and whoever you wish to be. The experiences in creation are endless. The knowledge of this – and not just that the experiences are endless, but so too is the part of creation having the experience – is heaven. This knowledge says that there is truly no end. There is no death. Creation – you – continue on and on and on. There is no need to fear "getting it wrong." There is no need to fear "death." A life lived with the full knowing of these concepts is a life which may be enjoyed and lived to the fullest. You know you're here to experience what it is like to be individually and distinctly you, and you know that you will go on and on forever, but your experience of you will be a continuous expansion. If you forget in this life and have a miserable time, you have the chance to experience another and another and another. Ultimately, that is what religion serves to tell mankind: You don't ever stop. There is Joy. There is Peace. There is Love.

Sometimes, the illusion is just too strong though, and the institution becomes greater than the people who built it and on whose shoulders it sits.

That was actually really awesome, but can we get back to sexuality?

Yes, so the male and the female body serve as mansions in this house, just as planets help to make up the universe. You wouldn't really say though that the universe is a planet, would you?

That seems like a bad example when you're trying to illustrate the point that everything is one.

We're breaking down the individual points so that the greater picture can be seen. You can't learn math without first learning about numbers, just as you can't spell unless you have an alphabet. So too can you not fully experience God and what it is to be whole unless you've experienced the sum parts of God. That's not to say however that male and female are actually separate.

Okay, back to oneness?

Indeed. Male and female have come to embody more than just descriptions of a human body. They've taken on all kinds of definitions and roles – and as we said to you the other day, "Expansion can come through letting go of definition as well as reveling in it." In truthfulness, the male and female body have within them – rather each individual aspect has within itself – male and female energy, because there is no "male" and "female" energy; there is only energy.

Huh?

A body may have a certain sexualized, categorized set of genitalia and chromosomes, but

147

that is simply the decorating style of the individual inhabiting the body. Think of it in terms of buying a home. Some people chose A-frames. Some people buy one-story. Some people want brick, others want wood. Some people buy one and then decide they would have rather bought another. Other people paint their houses, plant trees, constantly redecorate. It's the same thing with a body.

You choose a gender based on the experiences you wish to have... that kind of takes the charge out of all the sex stuff you wanted to ask, doesn't it?

Yup.

You're dying to get into it. Go ahead.

Okay, well I want to

(*Let's Talk About Sex* begins playing)

Lol, yes. Let's talk about sex. Why does religion talk so much about sex?

It doesn't. People do.

Sex is often a feared or taboo subject simply because again, the idea of living life for the experience and the love are really foreign concepts. People have entrained themselves with the notion that someone else has to be pleased – a church, a god, a parent, a sibling, even the mind itself. Interestingly enough, this again goes back to feeling.

Well, for example, how can living a life in the closet feel good?

You're getting into judgments with regard to feelings. Remember, if someone is in the closet, they have a reason. On the surface, it's a much more charged issue than playing a game, but think back to the terms we discussed earlier.

Can we use you for example?

Sure.

You don't define yourself sexually, correct?

I suppose.

So, even the definition of non-definition is too much of a commitment. Do you know why?

Yes. I spent so much of my life feeling boxed in that I'd rather just ignore labels.

You realize that by ignoring something, you are still paying attention to it, right?

I didn't mean it that way.

Yes, and no. Had you said, "I find myself attracted to people of both sexes," that might have been not ignoring. Refusing to even commit to a statement like that pretty much energetically says, "Don't touch that. It's still bruised."

Okay, but what does this have to do with...

149

Breathe. Trust us. This isn't about you (and it is). Just chill.

Wha-wha. Okay. Go....

I am Self Love.

You started to write "I am Divine Love." This is crucial to so many people – whether it's with regard to physical sex, thoughts about sex, or in a larger way, the energy of creation itself (which applies to jobs, money, everything in your life). You started to write this because right when you started to feel into sex, you pulled in all of the stories you were taught and the shame and "wrongness" of who you are. So you split. You felt like something was wrong with you, and you turned outside – hence moving from the term "self" to the term "divine." In other words, "I'm sorry oh essence of something greater and more compassionate than me. Please love me." Really, you were asking yourself to love you and accept you. Can you do that?

Yes.

It feels hard though, doesn't it?

Yes.

Why?

I don't know.

It feels hard because you don't know everything we've been talking about. You're still – even if it's just a little bit – hanging on to the misunderstandings of the parables instead of knowing what Jesus and all the rest really meant. You still feel like you've gotten it wrong somehow. You haven't. Your life doesn't look like other people's lives because it's not theirs. It's yours. It just seems like such a big deal because it's "life!" The truth is, it's no bigger a deal than ordering lasagna, and then eating it in a room full of people eating Brussels sprouts.

You kind of lost me.

You like lasagna, right?

I love it. I Garfield that shit up.

So if you were starving, and you really wanted lasagna, and you then got lasagna, would it matter if the person next to you hated lasagna?

Do I know the person? Are they sitting with me?

What you really mean by that is, "Do they have any influence or control over me?" and the answer, as always is, "Only if you let them." But for this example, we're going to say that you are 100 per cent, totally in your power.

Awesome. Then no. I'd chow down.

Well, sex – with regard to sexual preference –
can be explained like this: you've just ordered what
you want and found yourself in a room full of people
all eating Brussels sprouts. They are also
vegetarians, and there is meat in your lasagna.

Yeah, that might be uncomfortable.

Now walk past them into another room where
you discover there is an entire party going on
dedicated to lasagna and how awesome it is. Which
room would you rather be in?

The lasagna room!

Sexually speaking, religion to you is the Brussels
sprouts room.

Now, we'll go a little further. Are you okay with
this?

I'm actually sweating.

You're burning energy. You want to keep going?

Yes.

Your whole family is in the room with the
Brussels Sprouts. All of your friends are in the room
with the Brussels sprouts. If it were really about the
food, you'd just say, "Hey guys. I'm going to go eat
in there, and I'll see you later."

Not that I'm trying to push away this topic, but how does this relate to genetic religion, etc?

You exist as an individual aspect of source. Your place of origin – indeed your true eternal place of being – is Source. As you've individualized over and over and over (like a stem-cell splitting over and over and over), you've played many roles. You've chosen many paths. Indeed, your gender, your sexual preference, your hair color, skin color, life experiences, place of birth, social status, etc, have all been chosen paths. You've wanted to explore the ins and the outs (pun intended, lighten up!) of life and the myriad positionalities these choices provide. Underneath all of the costumes and identities, remains your true nature. From the perspective of being separate, you've remembered there is a "whole" to return to. Thus, religion was born: a way to live a structured, safe life, wherein oneness with god or the self or the community or the family, etc. could be achieved. Your true genetic religion is the recognition – the re-cognition – that you are Source. As we discussed earlier with regard to the language of computer codes, consciousness evolves to new understandings. Jesus knew this. Buddha knew this. All great teachers knew this – and still do.

You thought we were going to talk about genetic religion with regard to programming and dna, but the truth is, that's all Brussels Sprouts. Your true Genesis is Source.

You titled the chapter as you did because on a deeper level, you knew that your "last hurdle" is being able to leave your attachment to the Brussels sprouts room. Sexuality – in all of its various meanings – can be lasagna, or it can be Brussels sprouts. The choice is up to you.

So, if "sexuality" is an aspect of Creation as a whole, and we know that in reality, everything is one, you can see how important it is to always choose yourself, to always choose Self-love. You can love your self out of any fear. So often, you sit in the metaphorical room full of Brussels Sprouts and pretend to belong. You eventually give up the idea of ever eating what you want, and you start eating what everyone else is eating. Then, you get mad and angry whenever you see someone pass this room by for a room full of people who celebrate their choice to express their joy. This is a really simple look at what goes on in the world with respect to war, inequality, etc. "If I suffer, you must suffer."

The truth is, no one needs to suffer. This isn't a socialist statement. This isn't a politically motivated statement. It's a truth. Like any truth, people simply have to commit to knowing it and take it as fact.

154

Once mankind starts living with this knowing, then everyone is free to live and love as they see fit.

I didn't expect myself to go here, but I remember saying something like this to my mom one time, and she said something along the lines of, "There has to be a system. There have to be rewards for people who do good, and punishment for people who do bad. Otherwise, what is to stop everyone from doing evil?

Well, you can see the myriad of beliefs at play in those words. When we speak of freedom of the self, we mean freedom of the Self – freedom of Source, which is total love. This is the highest way we can communicate the idea, but it is no different than the commandment in all religions to love god and love thy neighbor as thyself.

What if I don't love myself?

Indeed, many people don't, and how can they love their neighbor when they don't truly love themselves? This is the notion behind your mother's argument of limitation. In truth, our words are meant to remind, to inspire the Self to reclaim the self – and vice versa – and to be all that it is meant to be – to experience the love and divine nature of Self.

What we are truly saying is: Choose Life.

"I am the resurrection."

One cannot resurrect unless one dies. The death that we are talking about here with regard to genetic religion is literally a death of self – but through death is rebirth. Through death is salvation, and this death is not necessarily a physical death. This idea of day by day crucifying yourself is not a literal call to self-annihilation. It is a call to be ever mindful of the human mind – of the idea of separation. As human beings, you will all suffer doubt from time to time. As your friend recently said to you after you took on a new business venture, "If you weren't nervous and scared, I'd be worried you were broken." Nervous and scared aren't "bad" emotions, they are just parts of the ride. They become "negative" only when you forget that there is a larger unfolding taking place – a larger metamorphosis – and this is what was meant by resurrecting the self. Resurrect the mind. Resurrect the heart. Crucify the doubts.

"Let go and let God, remember?"

God has just been attached and collapsed with the human mind, and this is the genetic religion that we are asking mankind to give up. Give up the devotion to mistrusting one another. Give up the devotion to mistrusting the Self. Be the divine spark in action everywhere, and if you slip, forgive yourself. So often people turn the other cheek to others and then stick around for more. That's not what was meant.

156

Turn the other cheek, forgive, and move on. Love your enemies. Forgive them. They are you. But if you can't see that clearly from where you are, move! Change your perspective. Change your perception. Yes, turn the other cheek, but learn from what's happening. The crux of that statement was "don't reward wrong with wrong," not, "be a martyr."

Create a better world, that's what we are saying to you. Create an ever expanding love-filled self. Love yourself as much as you possibly can. Love others as yourself. Release devotion to superior, inferior, right, wrong, etc, and reprogram the genetics of mankind with love.

While we're on the subject of release and religion, claim I am Divine Love, and truly let yourself enter a space with no past, no future, and no present other than what is: Divine Grace and love.

I'd like to actually take this opprtunity to talk a litle bit about grace.

Okay.

Well, up until quite recently, I thought of grace as a negative aspect of forgiveness.

How could forgiveness hold a negative aspect?

I suppose it couldn't...

Unless you believe it does.

157

I saw grace as something that was given, yet not deserved. In otherwords, "Amazing grace... that saved a wretch like me."

Well, we know you weren't quite prepared for this answer, but think of it like this, that "wretch" is the part of your consciousness that was choosing to play the game of not only separation, but desolation.

What do you mean desolation?

Is there any space more desolate than one where God, Love, indeed hope itself is perceived as gone? You see, in a place of limited consciousness, of limiting belief systems, of Self – capital S – limitation and separation, grace would simply be the overpowering aspects of love. Grace in this instance would be the outpouring of universal love made manifest, available, and accessible when one least expected it.

I feel like that doesn't necessarily go with the narrative you've been teaching. If we all create our own lives according to our own beliefs, how could love enter a place where there is a belief that says, "love can't come here?"

We'll let you in on a little secret: In the end, so to speak, love is always known. Even in the darkest hours of individualized existence, love is the thing making that separation possible. Love is the

158

backbone of every presence, whether that presence accepts the love or not. Love says, you are free to choose, but love also persists, and when an individualized life ends, love is once again known.

What about people who claim to have died and experienced hell? Can we talk a little bit about that? If love always conquers, how can you explain some people's accounts of having "died and gone to hell."

It's the same as accounting for those who have "temporarily died and gone to heaven," or those who have seen "the light at the end of the tunnel."

Is there a light? Yes. Is there a heaven? Yes. Is there a hell? Well, no, but yes.

What do you mean?

Heaven and hell, in so much as you understand them (according to the traditional religious ideology) exist… and they don't.

They exist in that they are beliefs being experienced. They are mass beliefs, and they are individual beliefs. This isn't something we've touched upon very much in our conversations, the idea of mass beliefs, but equate it to the idea of a school of fish. A school travels together. They are energetically in a pact with one another. Well, religious dogma is a sort of pact as well. This is where archetypes come into play. There are many

159

different ideas of what heaven and hell are, yet, on a large scale, the concept is pretty well fleshed out.

Mass beliefs are only as important as the individual participating in the manifested belief structure believes them to be. This is one of the reasons that within almost all religious systems, there is a "way out." There is always that one being who was able to transcend and gain what is perceived as a super-human understanding of God and apply that understanding and knowing in miraculous and transcendent ways.

The thing is, the only things that needs to be transcended are the beliefs that are keeping the self in a state of unconscious awareness wherein the relation to the divine – as the divine – is known.

Think of it like this: in every culture, there are rules…

I just had a funny thought. It's the opening lines from the movie Varsity Blues, "In West Caanan, Texas, there are rules…"

Exactly. In life, you perceive there are rules. There are things you have to do to stay alive, right? Science of Survival – it's taught very early on. Rules seem to govern the mind, but in the ultimate reality, rules are of the mind.

Again, I go to the admonition, "Be in the world, not of it."

It's not an admonition; it's really a great truth and direction.

Live here on this plane, in this place, and enjoy it, but know that this isn't the ultimate reality. There are so many other experiences to be had on so many planes, and you're in truth, having them even now as we speak. Just don't take life so seriously. Lots of people are so attached to taking things personally, and the truth is, if you could see things from our perspective, you would know that life is everywhere; it is continuous. It is so vast. There is so much life available to all. This one singular experience is but a small little spec – a piece of the hologram if you will.

Ah, back to book one!

Right. Everything is here now, and everything that is here now is also a contained whole that is contained by an even larger whole. Life just seems like it's all about this one existence in human form, and whatever you do here and now, decides your fate forever. Or in other belief systems, here and now is it, and when you leave this physical existence, that's it; lights out forever. Both can be experienced to an extent.

161

As a whole, you can leave this life and say, "Okay. I did that. It was fun, and now I'm on to something else." Or, you can take things from this life that you enjoyed, and create more experiences based on that joy.

It's like your "gift." Those quotation marks were yours, by the way, not ours. It's kind of funny how you spent all your life knowing you could do these awesome things, yet you pretended to be afraid of them. We would have called them abilities – because they are things you are able to do. End of story. Everyone has the capability.

Where was this going?

Well, you connected with someone on a level you'd never experienced consciously in this existence. You two were able to literally share dreams. There was all kinds of magic in your relationship, and when that relationship ended, you came to the conclusion that life was unfair, and you hated your abilities, and you sat around and pouted for almost two years.

Wow. Don't hold back, lol.

Well, you did. The truth that you now know is it was you the whole time. You were opening up to her, and it felt like it was her, but it was you. It was the expansion that love brought that moved you into

162

a place of trying to ride your psychic bike without the training wheels. Then, you fell over and kicked the metaphorical bike. You now know that you can take all of those good things you learned, and apply them to the next relationship. You just have to let go of the baggage that you associate with the gifts.

Lots of people struggle with this concept, just in different ways. They get put down as children, and they never recover. They lose a job and they never again regain their self worth. The truth is, in all of these instances, a choice was made that went something along the lines of, "That hurt, and I don't ever want to experience that again," so, the baby goes out with the bath water, as you say.

Now, Karmically speaking, and we're going to get more into this in just a moment, you're holding a little of this energy because you're basically saying, "Don't go there," which is a bit like saying, "Don't think of a pink elephant." Even if you manage not to think of one, you're still processing avoidance – which only serves to perpetuate the energy you're trying to "escape" from.

Interesting. You started with the notion that we have the choice to move on in the next life, but isn't that kind of negated by what you just said?

Down the hole we go!

The easy answer is, "no." What we're saying to you is, complete your tasks. If you know you don't want to relive the pain of the past relationship, let go completely of that story. Keep the good things, but don't haul them around still linked to the negativity you placed upon them.

This is why we placed so much emphasis in the first book around letting go of stories. That doesn't mean lobotomize yourself. It means learn to love everything. Learn to be in the moment. Use the tools you have acquired through this experience to help better the experience so that when it's over, you can look back and say, "I completed everything in that life that I wished to complete" or "I would like to take these gifts and use them in this other way." You can even go back and use them in the same ways if you prefer. There isn't a right or a wrong. We're just showing you how to move beyond the realm of what you call karma.

The easiest way to keep repeating a pattern is to never escape the pattern.

Bring it home for me.

Well, religion is a mass pattern. If people could take all the good from religion, and leave all the bad – and we say that not as if there are right and wrong choices, but if they could take away only the love, then humanity would truly ascend over night.

I almost didn't write that word, "ascend." I wanted to write change.

Claim divine love around that.

See, there is a story in the mass system that no one is allowed to leave. No one is allowed to ascend. There is always something you have to pay for, and even if you happen to "get it right," you're still going to die. This is why reincarnation and life after death have found places within these systems. There has to be some kind of hope. But the thing is, that hope is always someplace else. It's always at another time, and the thing is, mankind has only now – always.

Yes, when you die, a myriad of new experiences are present, but how great to see the kingdom truly at hand now?

In order to attain this, consciousness must expand. This is why we used the term "ascend." In mythology, the term usually means that someone has lifted from this plane of existence and into the next while fully embodied, and because human beings fear death so much, all of the emphasis has been put on "embodied." Expansion then gave way to "not dying," which is a much lower vibration. You didn't come here to live forever. We know that is a touchy thing to say to some people, but it's true. You didn't. The smaller, separated consciousness may argue that point, but eventually, the human body dies. It can certainly be maintained and kept for longer and longer periods of time, but eventually, the larger you that you really are, says "lets jump!"

As you said that, I heard the song "Instant Kharma" start playing in my head.

In a manner of speaking, life *is* instant karma, because everything you experience, everything you create, is being experienced and created right now. You can change a thought instantly, and thus, you can change an experience. Each moment of experience is the catalyst for what you think of as the "next" experience, but all you're ever experiencing is the now. Even when you have things like post traumatic stress where emotions or thoughts are triggered by "past" events, what you are experiencing is "that" moment re-played in the moment of now.

That brings up an interesting topic… something I think a lot of people will be interested in discussing.

My little sister, the psychologist, called me this morning to talk a little bit about the topic of forgiveness, and she mentioned what I think is an old AA quote, "Holding onto resentment is like taking poison with the hopes that it will harm someone else." I feel like holding onto grudges, can sometimes do the same thing.

Well, this is an important subject to address, especially on the heels of discussing karma, because the idea of karma is that you are paying for some deed or misdeed – or that you are earning points or demerits for the future based on what you are doing right now.

In so much as creation is always occurring in the present, this is true. If you're wounded, and you continue to pick at the wound, it will not heal. At the same time, if you fail to dress the wound or treat it, it has the potential to fester and rot. This happens a lot with regard to emotional wounds and relationships – both with self and "others."

This is instant karma; it's also what's behind the saying, "Judge not lest ye be judged." You see, most people think of karma as something they have that is between them and someone else. It's looked at as a weighted return against the collected energy expended (or not expended in some cases) by the individual. What most people don't realize is, they are in full control of their own karma. They can drop lifetimes of beliefs and karmic ties in an instant should they choose to allow themselves to do so.

Then why wouldn't they?

The answer is simply that they don't love themselves enough, and they don't love themselves enough, because there is something in them that says, "You deserve this thing that is happening." That's really what karma is: it's the belief that you've done something to deserve the present condition." The truth is you have done something: you've created a belief.

That's way too easy.

If you are god, who or what else is there to blame?

We've been down this road in great detail in the last book (Love, Life, God: The Journey of Creation).

Yep. Accept the fact that you are creation, and as creation, you have to take on the responsibility of forgiving yourself. If you can do that, you'll never be a victim.

Now, we would also add that forgiveness is a wonderful step, but beyond forgiveness – at least in terms of self – is the notion of self-denial. You've been taught to sacrifice your self – sacrifice the flesh to honor god. You then "stray," and feel the need to be forgiven to be loved. This is all very basic child psychology. There is inherent in most people a need to be loved. That need exists because somewhere, someplace, there is a message or belief in them that says, "I am not worthy of love," I am not loved enough," or "My own nature is so vile, that only

168

through Divine forgiveness and grace do I belong" –
and even then, after divine grace and forgiveness has
been "asked for," most people still carry around the
belief that they don't belong in a loving relationship
with creation. They need to be over seen. They need
to be punished. It's a game people play, and this
material is coming out so that those who wish to
stop the game may see it for what it is and stop
playing.

The words "Love thy God with all thy heart, and
Love thy neighbor as thyself" came directly from
Jesus Himself. Buddha posed the question, "All
wrong-doing arises because of mind. If mind is
transformed, can wrong-doing remain?

The answer is "no."

*You answered my question before I asked it. I
was going to relate this to crime and acts of
violation.*

All crime, all hatred, all misguided energy that
wishes to hurt another is a violation of one's own
divine Self. Again, we've spoken about this topic in
great detail in the previous book. We've shown you
exactly how these situations arise as well as why and
how to create anew.

The truth is, you can only truly allow the divine Self that you are to show through when you have fully forgiven.

Well, we've talked about forgiving ourselves, but what about forgiving other? You mentioned the quote about "Judge not..."

When you judge anyone, you judge your self, because you create a scale of comparison. You create a black/right, right/wrong system of duality that you lock yourself into. You are in a position to judge only in a corollary way. In this manner, you set yourself up to be judged by your own mind – and because the judge is your own mind, you will carry the sentence with you as long as the system of judgment remains in place.

As far as forgiving others, again, you don't "turn the other cheek" out of respect or duty, you turn the other cheek because as the eternal rule states, "hatred does not cease by hatred, but only by love." Many people have lived many lifetimes with the intention of "I will incarnate and prove to myself that I can love all. I will turn the other cheek, and I will be principled at all times." In this way, the individual has created karma with the Self. The individual keeps coming back to prove the ability to live and let live only to be caught up in human emotion. The trick is not to be inhuman, but to

170

forgive yourself and others when they falter, and to then move on. Forgive yourself when you falter. If you need to get mad in order to release an energy that has been pent up, get mad. If you have a belief that getting mad is wrong, well, you're creating karma as you call it, because you're subscribing to the belief that being mad is wrong while being in a human body. Your resistance to getting mad creates an opportunity to experience anger and grow beyond your limitation in a healthy way, yet the belief in the wrongness of the self stifles the energy, and as a result, you keep creating more and more situations wherein it is possible to get mad and "let it all out." Only because of this belief that being mad is wrong, you never let it out, so it builds, and builds, and builds. That energy has to go somewhere. It becomes destructive in many people because it causes further emotions that are deemed as "bad." Eventually, what might have manifested in a scream becomes a crash or a fight or a giant weather event.

Weather event?

Absolutly. Water, air, people: everything is energy. Everything is inter-connected.

On one level, you have to know that everyone creates their own reality, and on another, you have to understand your feelings – or let go of the need to understand them. Let go of the need to judge them.

Well, I have to play devil's advocate…

Indeed, there is another belief. We just said that all wrong doing is of the mind, but in truth, there is no wrong doing. There is only doing. That is a morally outrageous statement, but morals only exist in a place where immorality also exists. In a state of Divine love – which is the state we constantly refer to, there is no immorality or morality; there is only love. There is only oneness.

The Bible had it right: Salvation lies within forgiveness, but understand that it is not Jesus who needs to forgive you; it is you.

I am divine love.

Very well. Let's move on.

Chapter 9

Born Again

You love titling these chapters don't you?

Yep. I sure do.

Well, this is actually a great title, because we're asking you to be born again in every moment. In the Christian sense, being "born again" means that you are saved. Your sins have been forgiven, and you are born as a new creation in the eyes of God. In other religions, they take being born again as a literal event – reincarnation. Both meanings are quite appropriate.

Meaning..?

Well, let's look at the concept of sin. To sin literally means to separate from God. We know that a lot of people say it means "to miss the mark," but honestly, there is no mark.

Which, again, we discussed in book one.

Correct. You're not "here" to do or not do any one particular thing. You're here to expand. The end. Anything else is a story. Expansion is actually a kind of story as well, which is why we'd like to

claim Divine love and expansion around
"expansion." We'll change our story once again.

I am Divine Love.

When you say it, really feel it. Feel what it means
to BE Divine Love. You're not saying I am loved by
the divine. You are saying to the Divine, "We are
one. I am you. You are me. You are the Self that I
am." If that's scary, you don't need to know why,
simply make the choice to let go of whatever ideas
and beliefs you have that are causing the fear.
Choose to allow yourself to be safe in making that
claim. Direct your energy to direct The Energy to
direct your energy.

Huh?

Think of it like standing in front of a mirror, only
you get to direct the mirror. It will mirror back to
you whatever you tell it to mirror back, and you then
become the thing that is mirrored.

How does this relate to being born again?

Well, in the traditional sense, whether through
salvation or reincarnation, being born again, brings
about a new slate. We're here to tell you that you
can be a new slate any time you wish. All you have
to do – and we say all knowing full well that this
seems like a big thing to you – is forgive yourself
(let go of whatever separates you from god) and then

174

allow the support of the universe to come in and follow your direction.

Unfortunately, a lot of people do the first thing, and then they direct the universe to keep them coming back for more by not allowing the support. When the universe doesn't "follow through," they fall back into the parent-child relationship and they assume they've done something wrong. They feel separated, and thus, the cycle of reparations begins all over again.

Why? Why would people not allow the support?

People fear their own power. Everyone has been taught to fear everyone "else." "Human nature" is portrayed as this vile thing that will always seek to dominate others and seek its own power. In truth, this is just a mass belief system playing out.

In other words, as we perceive, so it is.

As you expect, so it is. As you allow, so it is. You only allow – in most cases – what you know. You allow the expected. Something new comes along, and you go, "I'm not sure about you…" The truth is, you've been asking, you just need to allow.

Speaking of, there are no coincidences in the Universe. You just stepped away to answer your phone.

I did. A friend called me in tears.

You literally just went over everything we've been talking about in the last chapter with her. Can you explain what was going on?

Sure. Her boyfriend of many years ran across one of her old journals from eight years ago and read it. She was freaking out. Basically, she felt like she had done some really bad stuff in her past, and she was scared out of her mind that he was going to leave her now that he knew some of the things she had done in her youth.

Well, she's freaking out because right now she's in that, "I'm not sure about you" phase. She thinks she's not sure about being known by him, but really, she's not sure about deserving love no matter what. She's not sure she can be loved for all of who she is. This is really the basis for the creation of religion. There is a need to be known at the very deepest level of being, yet many people feel shame or remorse about things they've done or even thoughts they've thought. They are not able to forgive themselves directly, so they give this power over to God – capital G, outside power – and they ask God to forgive them. In return for forgiveness, which they need in order to be loved, they pledge allegiance to whatever commandments and ideals "God" lays out. Religion has been self-serving in that it has allowed

176

people to forgive themselves in absentia. They've been able to move on with their lives and overcome these giant mental, emotional, chemical, physical, etc, blocks, but the truth is, there was no outside power. The power – the kingdom, as it were – was within. "God" just became the mechanism through which they could allow. What we're asking consciousness to do now, is to allow Self. Allow back in the support and sovereignty of the Divine Self.

Many times, people dismiss this help because it feels foreign. The girl on the phone didn't realize it, but she had a real desire to be known on all levels, so this incident wasn't so much about him rejecting her or not rejecting her, but about her looking at the past, owning it, and acknowledging that she is still worthy of love. It is about her knowing fully who she was – and in this case, who she no longer is – and that she is fully deserving of Self Love. This is her chance to be born again. It is the chance for her relationship to be born again. Born again does not mean "born the same." Being born again is about changing. It is about letting go of a story – mostly, the story of not being worthy enough, not being loved, and not being one with the god that you are.

Being born again is also a story. It is a story born out of wanting to change – but as we said earlier, the thing about wanting is that it can often lead to more wanting. Let go of the story that you need to be born again, and simply be what you want to be right now. Let go of anything you are not in alignment with – rather, let go of anything that is not in alignment with you.

I thought we only created or attracted the things that we were in alignment with.

You do, but so many times you change your vibration while keeping a very tight grip on what that old vibration created.

I think I understand. This came up in a private session I did the other day.

A woman came to me who was with a man she didn't want to be with; yet, she felt bad about leaving him, and she didn't really want to do it even though they were no longer a match. She kept wanting to balance the energy around why they weren't a match, and what I told her was, "Think of it like this: He's a hot coal. You wanted warmth, so you brought him to you. You picked up the coal with your bare hands, and you got burned. You realized that the coal was too hot, and not what you actually wanted, but you were too afraid of being cold again to throw the coal away, so you just stood there getting burned, trying to balance the pain of being burned.

178

That's somewhat correct. We'd add that it was her mixed messages about what she wanted – warmth, as you put it – as well as her ability to be supported in a relationship that caused the "burning coal" to appear. But yes, she's ready in most regards for a space heater now, but her hands are still gripping the coal. She's got to put one down to pick up the other. Remember, you are energy in action. It's easy to remember the energy part, but sometimes people forget about the action. And as you said to her, she still needed to take action. They physically shared a home, so there will be some dealings between them after they split, yet they don't have to be huge emotional upheavals. This is something many people don't quite get.

Creation is the ever unfolding moment of now. If you're counting to ten using single increments, you'll need to follow a certain physical order or pattern.

In other words, one, two, three, etc… all the way to ten, right?

Right, but the increments don't have to be unpleasant. People don't have to get plugged in as they go. It is possible to carry out actions on the physical plain without becoming completely engrossed in the process.

Can you be specific?

Sure. She has asked him to leave. He won't leave. She might have to take some kind of action, and she knows this. Therefore, she doesn't need to make a huge production of getting him out. She knows he doesn't want to leave. It's not her job to change that. It is her job to accept it, and go about creating what she wants – NOT creating for him.

That's very specific, and I get it. It's not up to her how he feels or what he does, but what is up to her is what she does and how she handles it.

Exactly. This is true with all of creation, and when you can combine this knowledge with that of divine/Self love, there will no longer be any need for religion. There won't be the need for governments, for saviors, or for any "ruling" body, because everyone will be coming from a place of love, empowerment, and brotherhood.

What's empowering about a break-up?

Well in this specific case, there are a lot of victim vibrations that will come up and have the opportunity to be addressed. In general, what we're really talking about though is living in total integrity. When you can live in total truth, love, allowance, and integrity, and not fall into a place of victimization or fear, the world will move at a pace you've likely never experienced. You'll live hundreds of lifetimes in one life because you won't be attached to any one certain outcome or situation. You'll be able to experience so much more. You won't need to be born again, because you will be experiencing new births all the time. You'll be experiencing them from a place of evolution, love, and joy as opposed to a place of killing off the old. You won't have any desire to kill the old because you'll seamlessly flow ever into the new. This flow includes the transition of physical death.

We spoke so much about life in book one, but in speaking of life, we also spoke of death – because truly it is ALL life. Life never ends.

There is a verse in the Bible that states, "I am the way, the truth and the light. No man comes to the Father but by me." This was spoken by Jesus and is an allusion to the power and sovereignty of the I am presence and the God consciousness that is present and available to everyone. The only way to be one with the "Father," with all that you are, with Source, is literally to know who you are. To know this, is to know eternal life. To know this, is to have peace on earth. To know this, is to truly know, "All you need is love."

…And so we ask you, "Who do you say I AM?

Epilogue

In 2008, I began writing *Love, Life, God: the Journey of Creation* by asking one single, three worded question, "Who are you?!" How fitting, that all these years, many, many conversations later, Source is now asking the same question of us.

A lot has transpired on this journey with Source, much of which has been chronicled in my writing. I tried to be as forthcoming and honest about my own journey as I possibly could, and along the way, I noticed judgment came up quite a bit. I'd moved beyond judging others for the most part, but I hadn't quite gotten past judging myself. And it came up in the strangest ways.

In November of 2009, I was told by a doctor – wrongly - that I had M.S.

At the time, I simply walked out to my car and broke down in tears. I did not go to thoughts of love. I did not go to thoughts of divine grace or "I create my reality." I went to, "How the fuck am I going to be any good to anybody now?" I beat myself up repeatedly – which is funny now, because in looking back, I can see exactly why my body hurt so badly and why walking was such a problem. I felt like I'd been slammed into a wall, and in truth, spiritually, I had been.

I had spent the last year working my tail off in voice over. I'd also finished writing a humor book, *The Big E – Everything is Energy* with my wonderful healing partner,

183

actress Dee Wallace. I had never been so fully alive; yet, spiritually, I felt guilty, and now, I was being punished.

I had been judging myself for moving beyond what I perceived to be the typical and "correct" definition of God and for simply enjoying my life.

How dare I not worry? How dare I not be afraid of the government or this war or that horrible event seemingly looming on the horizon? Who was I to be so damn peaceful and happy?

Enter guilt and shame.

Every time I would claim, "I am Divine love," I felt judged because I was still holding that a part of the Divine wasn't so divine after all. It wasn't okay for me to shine my light in the presence of so much darkness. How dare I love myself? How dare I accept myself? I was still holding on to the idea that life was inherently wrong and needed to be repented for. I was still holding on to the idea that I was wrong because I didn't seem to fit into any one particular description or category. Most of all, I was still holding on to religion.

I talk in book one about collapsed beliefs, and I have to say I didn't fully grasp the concept until the shit in my life metaphorically hit the fan. There I was, on hold for a half million dollar job, getting ready to celebrate the holidays with my family, and I could barely walk. How embarrassing.

I kept thinking to myself, "who would want to publish a book about creation and healing by a guy who can't even get out of bed? What kind of sick joke is this?"

I actually refused to write after that. Source asked me many times to return to the keyboard, and I would not. I tried to barter. "Make me better, and I'll keep going."

Does that sound familiar?

Without even realizing it, I had fallen back into the story of conceptualizing God. I'd willingly walked into the story of having fallen from grace and being in need of redemption.

Now in truth, I had fallen: from my own grace.

It took about six weeks, another G.P., a neurologist, and a massive amount of testing to decide that I was being stupid. Ultimately, I realized that what was happening to my body was in fact exactly what Source had spoken so much about in book one: the manifestation of belief systems.

I have to confess though, that conclusion played out by way of a dream:

My best friend in the whole world had been trying to conceive for several months. A little upset that I had been able to pinpoint the time of conception, birth, and sex of a mutual friends baby (I knew she was pregnant before she did. In fact, I actually called her and told her the day after she conceived that she was pregnant), he asked me to plug his future into my subconscious and see what my dreams came up with.

Now, full disclosure: I'm not entirely sure how it worked, but it did. A few days later, I had a dream. The baby would be born in June. A few nights later, I had another dream. This time, it was as if I was the baby, and I was coming into being – literally being conceived – and somehow, I knew it was September. Then, just a few short months before my legs began wobbling and my motor skills began going wonky, I had a dream, peering several years into the future, where I was visiting them, and I saw their baby – who by now was an adorable little girl who appeared to be four or five years old.

Being my best friend, I told him all about the dreams. By the time I was having trouble getting around, they were ready to announce the sex of the baby. I told him it had better be a girl, because that was the only way I knew that I was going to be able to walk in the future (as I'd been perfectly healthy and happy in the dream).

Sure enough, they gathered their family and a few close friends and revealed that they were in fact having a baby girl – conceived exactly when I'd said, due exactly when I'd said.

That was enough proof for me. I very quickly snapped out of my bullshit and realized that I had it all wrong. I hadn't been "struck down" for doing something wrong. I was simply experiencing the physical manifestation of conflicting beliefs. My judgment had become physical, and instead of realizing there was a conflict somewhere in my being, I sat down in a huff and tried to give up.

186

Source had been trying to get me to the keyboard because what was coming up was directly related to beliefs about God and "the ultimate reality" that I was still holding onto.

As I returned to the dialogue, I was told to work on grounding, and so I did. I spent several months working on getting back into my body – literally. And as I did, my motor function returned. I thoroughly worked the principals I'd been teaching others for so many years, and once again, I began experiencing miracles in my own life.

The diagnosis was changed to migraine syndrome. Then it was changed again, and again, until finally, feeling perfectly fine, I simply told the doctor, "You know what, I'm good." That was two years ago, and I haven't had a problem since.

Now, that's not to say that I haven't had the occasional runny nose, but I'm much better now about taking the time and letting myself heal instead of beating myself up. If I need to say no to something, I say no. If I need to take time away, I take time away.

Recently, I needed a vacation, but I didn't feel like I could afford to leave town. I followed my instincts and left. When I returned, I had an audition for a role that had been cast in my absence, and was now being recast. The producers were only seeing people they hadn't seen while I was away. I wound up auditioning next to maybe 3 other people instead of the 100 or so I would have been mixed in with had I staid in town, and I got the job.

Life is full of moments like that. Not everyone will always get the job, and not everyone will have a serious medical trauma either. Whatever you create, there is a reason. Don't beat yourself up. Maybe getting pulled over kept you from getting in an accident. Maybe that job less kept you from a path you can't even imagine right now. Maybe that missed train was the Universe trying to deliver a way for you to meet your new mate while waiting on the platform.

Whatever happens, keep loving yourself. Don't feel like there is some mark you have to hit, some eternal bar to raise, or some past debt you must forever repay – but if you, don't beat yourself up.

All judgment is the product of a story, and in many ways, religion is the last great story. Divine Love does not need a story, because forever and always, it just is.

Live fearlessly in a limitless world.

About The Author

Jarrad Hewett is an incredibly gifted medium and healer who has worked with some of the biggest and most recognizable names in the Self Help and Spiritual movements.

As a spiritual conduit, he is able to see, hear, and feel energy, thus he is able to see the energetic makeup of all that exists - including perceived problems on this physical plane: be they money, relationships, health, etc.

Jarrad is the best-selling author of *Love, Life, God: The Journey of Creation*, as well as *The Big E - Everything is Energy*.

Through his writing, he seeks to help others reconnect with their own inner guidance, wisdom, and peace.

Jarrad's goal is to empower all of creation by sharing his personal humor and insight.

To book a private, contact Jarrad at everythingenergy@aol.com.

Notes

Notes

Notes

Notes

Notes

CPSIA information can be obtained at www.ICGtesting.com
Printed in the USA
LVOW130041241112

308405LV00001B/41/P